What Loving Parents Don't Say Out Loud

Intrusive Thoughts About Harming Your Baby: Why They Happen, What They Mean, and How to Recover

Maribel Quinn Dawson

This book is provided for general educational and informational purposes. It is not a diagnosis, psychotherapy, medical treatment, emergency service, or substitute for care from a qualified health professional. Individual results and treatment needs vary, and no outcome is guaranteed.

If you intend or plan to harm yourself or your baby, cannot maintain safety, experience hallucinations, fixed beliefs that others say are not true, severe confusion, marked mania or major behavioral change, or otherwise believe there is an immediate danger, seek urgent medical help through your local emergency or crisis service. Do not use this book to decide whether an emergency symptom is 'only OCD.'

Do not begin, stop, change, or taper psychiatric medication based on this book. Pregnancy and breastfeeding decisions require individualized review with an appropriately qualified prescriber. Safeguarding, confidentiality, and child-protection duties vary by jurisdiction and circumstance.

Names and scenarios in this book are composites created for teaching. They are not intended to portray identifiable individuals or misrepresent any person, clinician, service, or organization.

ISBN: 978-1-911838-73-9

Table of Contents

Preface

Perinatal obsessive-compulsive disorder can begin or worsen during pregnancy and after birth, and unwanted thoughts about infant harm are a recognized presentation. Those thoughts can also resemble, on the surface, symptoms that belong to very different and more urgent clinical pictures. That makes precision unusually important: the content of a thought matters, but so do the person's relationship to it, reality testing, intent, behavior, compulsions, mood, and ability to maintain safety.

An intrusive thought is an unwanted thought, image, impulse, urge, or doubt that enters awareness. In OCD, recurring obsessions become linked with compulsions such as checking, avoidance, reassurance seeking, rumination, confession, or testing. The content of a thought does not by itself determine diagnosis or risk. Postpartum psychosis is a different clinical condition that can involve delusions, hallucinations, severe confusion, marked mood disturbance, and rapidly changing behavior. Actual intent to harm, an inability to maintain safety, or symptoms suggesting psychosis require urgent professional assessment. A book cannot make that assessment.

The gap this book addresses is narrower than general postpartum anxiety. Many parents can find information about worry, sleep, feeding, or broad maternal wellness while still struggling to find careful language for the thoughts they are most afraid to name. The same gap appears around disclosure. A parent may understand the phrase "intrusive thought" yet still have no idea what a clinician will ask, how obsessional phenomena differ from intent, or how safeguarding duties fit into a proper risk assessment.

This book provides a structured way to understand that problem without turning explanation into repeated reassurance. Its practical spine is the SAFE Return: Spot the obsession, Allow uncertainty,

Forego the compulsion, and Engage with real care. The method is a memory aid built from established ERP principles. It is not a new therapy, a diagnostic test, or an emergency protocol. The chapters also explain what a competent assessment considers, how ERP can be adapted to infant care and fragmented sleep, how partners can support treatment without becoming reassurance providers, and how medication questions belong in individualized perinatal medical care.

The primary reader is a pregnant or postpartum parent frightened by unwanted harm thoughts, especially a parent who has hidden the content. Partners and support people may also find the assessment and response language useful. The book does not promise that intrusive thoughts will disappear, that disclosure will produce one predictable outcome, or that self-help is sufficient for severe symptoms. Safeguarding law and service pathways differ by location, and medication decisions require a qualified prescriber.

The purpose is practical: help you describe what is happening accurately, recognize when urgent assessment is needed, understand the OCD cycle, seek appropriate care, and return more of your attention to ordinary parenting rather than repeated attempts to prove what a thought means.

Introduction: The Sentence You Cannot Say

There is a sentence many new parents can describe only by circling around it.

They can say that they feel anxious. They can say they are checking the baby too much, avoiding parts of the kitchen, asking their partner to take over bath time, or searching the same question again after everyone else has gone to bed. They may say that an image keeps appearing in their mind and that they hate it. What they cannot always say is the content.

The missing sentence may be, "I had a thought that I could hurt my baby."

It may be an image of intentional harm, a flash of sexual content that produces immediate disgust, or a sudden "what if" that feels so vivid the parent becomes afraid to be alone with the child. The parent may not want the thought. She may spend hours trying to prove that she does not want it. Still, the thought can feel like evidence.

That is the problem this book addresses.

Intrusive thoughts can be words, images, doubts, impulses, or urges that arrive without invitation. Many people experience unwanted mental content. During the perinatal period, thoughts about infant harm are especially common in research samples, and some parents develop obsessive-compulsive disorder, or OCD, around those thoughts (Hudak & Wisner, 2012; Hudepohl et al., 2022). A prospective study of 763 women found a weighted period prevalence of 7.8 percent during pregnancy and an estimated period prevalence of 16.9 percent across the postpartum follow-up when perinatal-specific symptoms were considered (Fairbrother et al., 2021). Those numbers do not tell you whether you have OCD. They do tell us that clinicians and families need language for a problem that is not rare.

The content can be frightening enough that the parent starts treating the thought as a warning. She checks her reactions. She avoids being alone with the baby. She moves household objects, rehearses memories, searches online, asks for reassurance, confesses the thought to her partner, and then asks whether the confession sounded suspicious. Each act may bring a small amount of relief. The relief does not last. The question returns.

OCD is not defined by one particular thought. It involves obsessions and compulsions that consume time, cause distress, or interfere with daily life. An obsession is a recurring unwanted thought, image, impulse, urge, or doubt. A compulsion is a behavior or mental act used to reduce distress, gain certainty, or prevent a feared event. Perinatal OCD often centers on the baby, but the same cycle can attach to contamination, accidental harm, intentional harm, sexual harm, health, religion, relationships, or other areas of responsibility (Royal College of Psychiatrists, n.d.).

This book is about one portion of that picture: unwanted harm thoughts in pregnancy and the first postnatal year.

It is also about a distinction that deserves careful treatment. An unwanted obsession is not the same clinical phenomenon as a delusion, hallucination, fixed false belief, severe confusion, mania, or an intention to harm. Postpartum psychosis is rare, severe, can develop rapidly, and requires urgent medical assessment (Toor et al., 2024; NICE, 2014/2020). Because infant-harm content can appear in both OCD and psychosis, content alone cannot settle the question. Clinicians look at the entire presentation, including reality testing, insight, mood, intent, planning, behavior, sleep, functioning, and other symptoms.

That distinction is one reason this book refuses two shortcuts.

The first shortcut is panic: "I had the thought, therefore I am dangerous."

The second is blanket reassurance: "I am upset by the thought, therefore nothing could ever be wrong."

Neither is a good risk assessment. This book will teach you why obsessional thoughts are clinically different from intention and psychosis, while also giving you clear signs that call for urgent professional help.

What Recovery Actually Means

If you have been measuring recovery by the absence of disturbing thoughts, you may have created an impossible job. A mind can produce strange, violent, sexual, blasphemous, absurd, tender, boring, and frightening material without asking permission. Trying to control every mental event can make you monitor your mind more closely, which gives the unwanted material more attention.

A more useful target is behavior.

Can you feed your baby without reviewing what every image means? Can you change a diaper without testing whether you felt the "right" emotion? Can you hand a kitchen tool to your partner because they need it, not because you are conducting a safety ritual? Can you tell a clinician what is happening without editing out the part you fear will sound terrible? Can you let a question remain unanswered long enough to return to real life?

For OCD, exposure and response prevention, usually called ERP, is a first-line psychological treatment. ERP involves approaching feared cues or uncertainty while reducing the compulsive responses that have been used to obtain relief or certainty (International OCD Foundation, n.d.). Perinatal experts recommend adapting established OCD treatment principles to pregnancy and postpartum care, while considering the practical and medical context of the perinatal period (Mulcahy et al., 2023; Hudepohl et al., 2022).

This book does not ask you to invent high-intensity exposures on your own. It gives you the logic of ERP and a small response tool that can be used alongside professional treatment.

That tool is the SAFE Return.

Spot the obsession. Notice that the mind has presented a threat question.

Allow uncertainty. Decline the demand to reach perfect certainty about what the thought "proves."

Forego the compulsion. Step away from the checking, reassurance, rumination, avoidance, confession, or testing that would provide temporary relief.

Engage with real care. Return to the next ordinary, proportionate parenting action while keeping normal safety practices.

The SAFE Return is not a diagnostic test. It is not an emergency plan. It is not a replacement for ERP with a trained clinician. It is a portable way to remember the direction of recovery when your mind is demanding an answer now.

The Question Behind the Question

A person with harm OCD may ask, "How can I know for certain that I would never hurt my baby?"

The understandable temptation is to answer that question directly and repeatedly. But OCD can turn certainty into a moving target. The answer that worked at breakfast may feel inadequate by lunch. A new detail appears. A memory feels strange. A physical sensation seems significant. The mind says, "Yes, but what about this?"

The treatment direction is different: learn to recognize when the demand for certainty is the trap.

That does not mean becoming careless. Babies need ordinary safety. Tired adults need support. Medical symptoms need medical care. Mental health emergencies need urgent assessment. The goal is not to ignore proportionate risk. It is to stop adding OCD safety rules whose real purpose is to make uncertainty disappear.

Throughout the book, **ordinary safety** means the same reasonable precautions you would use without OCD's demand for extra certainty. An **OCD safety rule** is an added restriction, check, ritual, or avoidance whose main function is to reduce obsessional doubt rather than address a proportionate real-world risk.

That distinction will matter when we discuss bath time, stairs, driving, household tasks, diapering, being alone with the baby, and sleep deprivation. It will also matter when we discuss disclosure. A clinician cannot responsibly decide risk from one sentence. Good assessment looks at the whole pattern.

If You Need Urgent Help

This is the part to read even if you want to skip ahead.

Seek urgent medical assessment if you are experiencing hallucinations, delusions or fixed beliefs that others say are not true, severe confusion, marked mania or extreme behavioral change, a felt command to harm, an intention or plan to harm yourself or your baby, or any situation in which you cannot keep yourself or your baby safe. NICE states that sudden symptoms suggesting postpartum psychosis require immediate specialist assessment, and describes postpartum psychosis as a condition that can become very severe quickly (NICE, 2014/2020). Toor and colleagues likewise describe postpartum psychosis as a psychiatric emergency requiring immediate medical attention (Toor et al., 2024).

If that is your situation, this book is not the next step. Urgent assessment is.

If your thoughts are unwanted, frightening, and linked to checking, reassurance, rumination, or avoidance, the chapters ahead can help you put accurate language around the pattern and prepare to seek OCD-informed care. A book still cannot determine your diagnosis or individual risk. That work belongs with a qualified clinician.

How to Use the Book When You Are Tired

You do not need a pristine hour and a notebook.

Read one section. Mark one sentence. Try one action. If a chapter makes you want to use it as a new reassurance source, notice that too. Re-reading the same paragraph ten times to obtain certainty can become part of the cycle, even when the paragraph is accurate.

The early chapters answer what the thought is and what it is not. Chapters 6 and 7 walk through disclosure and assessment because fear of telling someone is often its own crisis. Chapters 8 through 10 cover treatment and the SAFE Return. The later chapters apply the method to infant care, partners, sleep disruption, medication conversations, bonding, and relapse.

The central idea is simple enough to carry while your hands are full: you can respond to an intrusive thought as a mental event, take real safety seriously, and stop making perfect certainty the price of caring for your baby.

Chapter 1: The Thought You Won't Say

Maya was fastening the snaps on her daughter's sleeper when a violent image appeared in her mind. It lasted only a moment. Nothing in the room had changed. The baby kicked one foot free, made an impatient sound, and waited to be picked up.

Maya changed.

She set the baby down and studied her own hands. She replayed the image. Had it felt unwanted quickly enough? Had there been a fraction of a second before the fear arrived? She checked her body for anger. Then she checked for affection. When her partner came into the room, she handed over the baby and said she needed a minute.

That minute became an hour of mental review.

The first event was an intrusive thought. The next sixty minutes were an attempt to decide what the thought meant.

That distinction matters because a thought can be brief while the response to it becomes a system.

A Thought Is an Event, Not a Finding

An intrusive thought is an unwanted thought, image, impulse, urge, or doubt that enters awareness and feels disturbing or inconsistent with what you want. The word *intrusive* describes how the mental event arrives and is experienced. It does not describe a diagnosis by itself.

Pregnancy and new parenthood give the mind an enormous amount of new material. There is a small person whose safety matters, countless decisions that cannot be made with perfect certainty, and a body that may be recovering while sleep arrives in fragments. Research on perinatal OCD repeatedly notes that obsessions during this period often focus on harm to the infant (Hudak & Wisner, 2012; Hudepohl et al., 2022). The Royal College of Psychiatrists also lists unwanted images or thoughts of accidental, deliberate, violent, and sexual harm among recognized perinatal OCD presentations (Royal College of Psychiatrists, n.d.).

The existence of such content can feel shocking because people often assume the mind should reflect character in a clean, orderly way. If you love someone, your mind should produce only loving material. If you value safety, your mind should produce only safe images. If you have a violent image, perhaps some violent part of you wanted it.

That reasoning feels intuitive. It is also a poor way to understand involuntary thought.

A mind generates possibilities. It notices threats. It combines memories, sensations, words, pictures, and fears. Sometimes it produces material that is precisely the opposite of what a person wants. The arrival of a thought is therefore not the same thing as endorsing it.

This is not an instruction to repeat, "The thought means nothing," until you feel calm. That sentence can become reassurance if you use it to settle the question every time. A more durable response is narrower: *A thought occurred. I can choose what I do next.*

The Vividness Trap

Priya's intrusive thoughts were images rather than sentences. Because they looked clear in her mind, she treated the clarity as evidence.

"If I can picture it that easily," she thought, "there must be a reason."

The mind can create vivid material about many things that are not wanted, planned, or likely. Vividness tells you something about the sensory quality of an image. It does not, on its own, tell you why it appeared or what you will do.

OCD can turn this simple fact into another test. You may start comparing today's image with yesterday's. Was this one sharper? Did it stay longer? Did you feel less disgust? Did you move your hand before or after it appeared? That comparison feels investigative. Functionally, it can be a mental compulsion, because its purpose is to reach certainty about safety or identity.

A useful question is not, "How vivid was the thought?"

Ask instead, "What did I do because I needed to know what the vividness meant?"

That shift moves attention from uncontrollable mental content to a behavior you can change.

The Urge That Feels Different

Some readers will say, "Mine was not just a thought. It felt like an urge."

The word *urge* understandably raises the stakes. It can refer to a felt impulse, a physical sensation, a feared loss of control, or a genuine wish to act. Those are not interchangeable. A book cannot determine which one you are experiencing.

In OCD, people can experience unwanted urges and become intensely preoccupied with whether the urge was "real." They may then test it. They stand near a trigger and inspect their body. They imagine the feared action to see how it feels. They ask whether they felt resistance. They compare the sensation with an ordinary urge such as hunger.

The testing creates more data to test.

If you have an actual intention or plan to harm your baby, if you feel unable to control your behavior, or if you cannot maintain safety, seek urgent professional assessment. If what you are experiencing is unwanted and followed by repeated checking, avoidance, reassurance, or rumination, tell a qualified clinician that full pattern. Do not force yourself to decide the diagnosis privately.

The Moral Interrogation

Nia's mind did not ask whether the image was likely. It asked whether she was a good person.

She answered for hours.

She remembered volunteering in college. She remembered losing her temper with a sibling. She recalled a movie scene she had once watched without looking away. She compared how intensely she loved her baby on different days. She tried to reconstruct whether she had ever been cruel to an animal as a child.

This is one reason harm OCD can be so consuming. The feared catastrophe is not only, "What if something happens?" It can be, "What if this reveals who I really am?"

That question has no natural finish line. Human beings contain mixed emotions, irritated moments, strange memories, unchosen sensations, and imperfect reactions. If your standard is absolute proof of moral purity, every ordinary inconsistency becomes suspicious.

Thought-action fusion is a term used in cognitive models of OCD for a tendency to treat thoughts as unusually significant. One form involves feeling that thinking about an event makes it more likely. Another involves treating a thought as morally similar to carrying out the act (Shafran et al., 1996). Perinatal OCD can make this especially painful because the topic is a baby whose safety carries enormous moral weight.

The practical response is not to build a stronger character defense. It is to stop holding a trial each time the mind presents a piece of evidence.

Suppression Is Still Attention

Leah tried to solve the problem by banning the thought.

Whenever an image appeared, she said "stop" in her mind and replaced it with a picture of the baby smiling. She became skilled at noticing the first hint of the unwanted image, which meant she also became skilled at monitoring for it.

The thought seemed to appear more.

Research on thought suppression has long found rebound and monitoring effects in which efforts not to think a thought can make it more accessible under some conditions (Wegner, 1994). You do not need to conduct a thought-suppression experiment on yourself. The practical point is simpler: a policy of "this thought must never appear" requires you to keep checking whether it has appeared.

That is a lot of attention to give something you want to shrink in importance.

Allowing a thought to be present does not mean agreeing with it. It means ending the emergency procedure around its existence.

Try noticing the wording: "My mind produced that image."

Then return to the task in front of you.

You are not trying to achieve a serene internal state before you return. The return is the practice.

Common Does Not Mean Harmless to Your Life

There is a delicate point here. Unwanted intrusive thoughts about infant harm occur in many parents, including parents who do not meet criteria for OCD. Clinical and research literature describes them as common in the postpartum period (Hudak & Wisner, 2012; Hudepohl et al., 2022).

A frightened reader can turn "common" into a reassurance ritual.

"How common exactly? Is my version included? What percentage of people had my exact image? Did they have it as often as I do? Did they feel the same sensation?"

Now a prevalence statement has become a measuring device.

The point of prevalence information is to correct the false assumption that disturbing mental content automatically identifies a uniquely dangerous person. It cannot decide your diagnosis or individual risk. What matters clinically includes frequency, distress, time, impairment, compulsions, insight, intent, and the wider mental state.

A common phenomenon can still be disabling.

If you lose hours to rumination, cannot complete ordinary infant care, avoid being alone with your baby, or need repeated reassurance to get through the day, the impact deserves assessment even if the original mental event is common.

Secrecy Changes the Shape of the Problem

There is a difference between privacy and concealment driven by fear.

You are entitled to privacy. You do not owe acquaintances a list of intrusive thoughts. But when secrecy prevents you from giving a clinician the information needed to understand your symptoms, it can keep you trapped with your own interpretation.

A parent who says only, "I'm anxious," may receive general advice about rest and relaxation. A parent who says, "I have repeated unwanted images of intentionally harming my baby, I do not want them, and I spend two hours a day checking whether I might act on them," gives a very different clinical picture.

That sentence still does not dictate the outcome of an assessment. It does give the assessor useful information.

Chapter 6 will help you prepare that disclosure. For now, notice the reason you are editing the story. Is it ordinary privacy, or are you trying to make the thought sound less alarming because you fear the listener will mistake content for intent?

If it is the second, that fear belongs in the conversation too.

The First Thirty Seconds

When a thought arrives, the first thirty seconds often contain a choice point.

The old sequence may be:

Thought.

Shock.

Check whether you hated it.

Search memory.

Avoid the task.

Ask for reassurance.

Feel better briefly.

Notice another doubt.

The new sequence is deliberately less impressive:

Thought.

Notice.

Do not investigate.

Continue the ordinary task if it is safe to do so.

This is not full ERP. It is a first move away from compulsion.

Suppose you are changing your baby and an unwanted sexual image appears. Your mind says, "Why would a mother think that?" The compulsive answer may involve checking your body, searching online, replaying the moment, or asking a partner to finish diaper changes from now on.

A first response can be: "That is an intrusive thought. I do not have to solve its meaning right now."

Then continue the ordinary care task, unless there is a genuine reason unrelated to OCD that you cannot do so safely.

The sentence is not a magic phrase. If you repeat it forty times until you feel certain, it has become another ritual. Say it once if it helps you orient, then act.

The Difference Between Naming and Reassuring

OCD treatment often uses accurate psychoeducation. Accurate information matters. So does the function of how you use it.

Naming says, "This pattern resembles an obsession-compulsion loop, and I will discuss it with a qualified clinician."

Reassurance says, "I need to read the diagnostic explanation again until I feel completely certain that I am safe."

Naming opens the next appropriate action. Reassurance tries to close uncertainty.

This distinction will recur throughout the book. The same paragraph can be educational on Monday and compulsive on Tuesday depending on why you are reading it.

If you notice yourself returning to a section solely to get the feeling of certainty back, try waiting ten minutes before rereading. During those ten minutes, do something ordinary that matters: finish feeding, put laundry away, text the person who is bringing groceries, or sit on the floor while your baby plays.

You are practicing a new rule: information can guide action without becoming a guarantee.

When the Thought Is About You, Too

Harm OCD can include thoughts about the baby, yourself, a partner, or another child. Depression can also occur during pregnancy and postpartum, and suicidal thoughts require direct clinical attention. The presence of OCD does not rule out depression or another condition (Hudepohl et al., 2022).

If your intrusive content includes self-harm and you are unsure whether it is an unwanted obsession or a wish to die, do not use this book to decide alone. Tell a qualified professional what the thought is, whether you want it, whether you have intent or a plan, and whether you believe you can stay safe.

If you are in immediate danger, use emergency services.

The habit we are building in this chapter is not "all disturbing thoughts are OCD." It is "content alone is not enough, and I do not have to hide the information needed for proper assessment."

A Small Practice for Today

Choose one recent intrusive thought that you have already spent time analyzing.

Write, or say privately, one neutral sentence:

"I noticed an unwanted image about harm while I was feeding the baby."

Stop there.

Do not add, "and this proves..." or "but I would never..." Do not rate how bad it was. Do not explain why a good parent would not think it. You are practicing description without verdict.

Now name one response that followed.

"I searched for stories from other mothers for forty minutes."

Or:

"I asked my partner three times whether he trusted me."

Or:

"I avoided the stairs."

The second sentence is where your influence begins.

You may not be able to stop a thought from arriving. You can learn to change the repeated response that teaches your mind the thought is an emergency.

Principles to Remember

An intrusive thought is a mental event. Its presence is not the same as an intention, plan, or action. The more useful question is often not "Why did I think this?" but "What did I do next because I needed certainty?"

Vividness, disgust, numbness, or a strange physical sensation can all become material for checking. Treating those reactions as tests tends to create more tests.

Unwanted harm thoughts occur in perinatal OCD and also in parents who do not have OCD. Prevalence information can correct shame, but it cannot diagnose you or settle individual risk.

If you have intent, a plan, severe confusion, psychotic symptoms, or cannot keep yourself or your baby safe, seek urgent assessment. If your thoughts are unwanted and followed by compulsions or avoidance, give a clinician the full pattern.

For the next chapter, bring one question: not "How can I prove the thought means nothing?" but "What keeps the alarm running after the thought has already passed?"

Chapter 2: When a Thought Becomes OCD

Hannah's baby slept in a bassinet beside the bed. Hannah checked that the baby was breathing, lay down, then checked again.

The second check made sense to her because the first had not felt complete. She could not remember whether she had really looked at the baby's chest or merely thought she had. On the third check, she watched long enough to see several breaths. Then a new thought appeared: *What if I am watching the wrong thing?*

She placed a hand near the baby's nose.

Her partner asked whether anything was wrong.

"No," Hannah said. "I'm just being careful."

By dawn, careful had become a sequence of checks that no check could finish.

OCD often hides inside reasonable words. Careful. Responsible. Prepared. Clean. Certain. The behavior may look protective from the outside. The clue is what the behavior is being asked to accomplish.

Obsession, Distress, Compulsion, Relief

The basic OCD cycle is simple to draw and hard to live inside.

An obsession arrives.

Distress or uncertainty rises.

A compulsion is used to reduce that distress or prevent a feared outcome.

Relief follows.

The relief teaches the brain that the compulsion mattered.

The next obsession arrives with more authority.

A compulsion can be visible, such as checking, washing, arranging, asking questions, or avoiding a task. It can also be internal, such as reviewing a memory, repeating a phrase, checking whether you feel love, analyzing an image, praying in a rigid certainty-seeking way, or arguing with the thought.

Perinatal OCD reviews describe checking, avoidance, reassurance seeking, cleaning, and other rituals in response to obsessions about infant safety (Hudepohl et al., 2022). The Royal College of Psychiatrists similarly describes repeated checking, reassurance, mental rituals, and avoidance in perinatal OCD (Royal College of Psychiatrists, n.d.).

The form of the compulsion matters less than its job.

If the job is "make me certain that I am not dangerous," the mind can always ask for another round.

The Relief Test

Grace searched the internet after a thought about accidental harm. She told herself she was gathering information.

That description was partly true. Good information can guide good decisions.

The problem was the pattern. She searched the same phrases every evening. She skipped results that made her nervous. She read forum posts until she found one that matched her experience closely enough. She felt relief for twenty minutes. Then she wondered whether the person in the post had actually had the same kind of image.

Back she went.

One way to identify a possible compulsion is the relief test:

What feeling am I trying to get from this action?

If the answer is ordinary information needed for a decision, the action may be useful. If the answer is "I need certainty before I can move on," look more closely.

A second question is:

How long does the answer hold?

Information that solves a practical problem tends to remain solved unless circumstances change. Compulsive reassurance tends to expire.

This is not an absolute test. Human behavior is messy. The point is to notice function and repetition.

Overt Compulsions

Some compulsions are easy to see once you know what to look for.

You may check the baby far beyond the schedule recommended for ordinary care. You may repeatedly inspect your hands before picking the baby up, not because of a new contaminant but because the "clean enough" feeling will not arrive. You may ask your partner to supervise routine tasks that you can physically do safely. You may lock away ordinary household items solely to stop yourself from wondering what their presence means about you.

You may also arrange life around prevention of the thought itself. You take a longer route to avoid a staircase. You stop bathing the baby. You refuse to prepare food. You avoid being in the room during diaper changes. You keep another adult present every time you hold your child.

Avoidance can be especially deceptive because not doing something looks passive. In the OCD cycle, it can function as an active safety behavior: *If I never face this situation, I never have to learn whether I can tolerate the uncertainty.*

There are real situations in which a tired or medically unwell parent should hand over care. There are ordinary infant-safety practices everyone should follow. We will deal with that distinction in Chapter 11.

For now, ask whether the rule is proportionate to a real condition or whether it is designed to obtain a feeling of certainty.

Mental Compulsions

Mental compulsions are harder to identify because nobody can see you doing them.

Samira could feed her baby while conducting a full internal investigation.

Did I feel irritated before the thought?

Did the image come before I moved my hand?

Would I be this scared if I secretly wanted it?

Did I love her enough this morning?

Would a dangerous person ask these questions?

She could spend forty minutes answering without making a sound.

Rumination often masquerades as problem solving. A problem usually has a point at which new information lets you decide. Rumination keeps asking versions of a question that cannot be settled to OCD's standard.

Another mental compulsion is memory review. You may examine past moments for proof. Did you ever shove a sibling? Did you enjoy a violent movie? Did you resent pregnancy? Were you angry during a feeding? The review assumes that a perfectly safe person would have a perfectly clean history of thoughts, emotions, and reactions.

No human being can meet that standard.

You do not need to replace the review with a positive review. "Let me list all the times I was kind" still accepts the premise that your safety can be proved by an internal trial.

The response prevention is to end the trial.

Reassurance as a Shared Compulsion

Jordan told their partner every intrusive thought.

At first the disclosure felt freeing. Then Jordan began adding questions.

"That sounds like OCD, right?"

"You know I would never do anything, right?"

"Did I look weird when I said that?"

"Would you leave the baby with me?"

The partner answered patiently. Then Jordan needed the answers repeated in slightly different words.

Reassurance seeking is common in OCD because another person's confidence feels stronger than your own. The problem is not asking for help. The problem is turning another person into a certainty machine.

Support sounds like: "I can see that you're distressed. Let's use the plan you made with your therapist."

Compulsive reassurance sounds like: "Tell me again, with absolute certainty, that the thought proves nothing."

A partner can decline the second while still offering the first. Chapter 12 gives specific scripts.

Confession Can Be Reassurance Too

Confession has a special force in taboo-thought OCD.

You may feel an urgent need to tell your partner exactly what appeared in your mind, including every small variation, because withholding it feels dishonest. Once you tell them, you watch their face. If they remain calm, relief arrives.

Then another detail seems important.

"I forgot to tell you that I was frustrated with the crying ten minutes earlier."

Now you confess that too.

Disclosure to a clinician for assessment is not the same as compulsive confession. Neither is normal communication with a partner. The function and repetition matter. A useful disclosure gives information to someone who needs it. Compulsive confession is repeated to neutralize guilt or obtain a verdict about character.

Before confessing a detail for the third time, ask, "Does this person need the information to make a decision, or do I need their reaction to make me feel clean?"

If it is the second, delay.

Checking Feelings

A particularly painful compulsion in postpartum OCD is emotional checking.

You hold the baby and ask, "Do I feel love right now?"

You notice tiredness instead of warmth.

Panic rises.

You try the cuddle again.

Now you feel artificial because you are monitoring yourself. The lack of spontaneous warmth becomes more evidence.

Bonding does not require a constant internal state. Parents can feel tenderness, irritation, boredom, protectiveness, numbness, delight, grief, and exhaustion across the same day. Depression, anxiety, trauma, pain, feeding difficulties, and sleep disruption can also affect how someone feels.

If you turn bonding into a moment-by-moment test, ordinary variation becomes threatening.

For OCD, the response is not to manufacture the "correct" feeling. It is to stop grading each interaction.

You can perform a caring action without using the action as an exam.

Thought-Action Fusion

The phrase *thought-action fusion* describes beliefs that give thoughts unusual moral or predictive weight. In the original cognitive literature, researchers distinguished a moral form, in which having an unacceptable thought feels morally equivalent to doing something wrong, and a likelihood form, in which thinking about an event feels as if it can make the event more likely (Shafran et al., 1996).

In perinatal harm OCD, the moral form can be brutal.

"If a loving mother would never think this, and I thought it, what does that make me?"

The reasoning contains a hidden assumption: loving people control all spontaneous mental content.

They do not.

But again, be careful how you use that sentence. If you repeat "loving people have weird thoughts" every time the obsession appears, you may turn accurate psychoeducation into a ritual.

The treatment target is the fusion itself. The thought is allowed to be a thought. Your moral behavior is expressed through what you intentionally do, how you respond to real responsibilities, and whether you seek appropriate help when needed. You do not have to establish a perfect internal record before you are allowed to act according to your values.

The "Just Once" Problem

OCD rarely announces, "Please perform a compulsion that will train me to return."

It says, "Check just once."

The first check may even be appropriate. You confirm that the bathwater temperature is safe. You lock a cabinet. You follow safe-sleep guidance. These are ordinary actions with a stopping rule.

Then uncertainty appears.

"Maybe I did it wrong."

The second action is not driven by new evidence. It is driven by the feeling that the first action did not produce certainty.

This is where ordinary safety becomes an OCD safety rule.

A stopping rule is useful. For an ordinary task, decide in advance what "done" means based on proportionate guidance, not on the disappearance of anxiety.

For example: "I checked the buckle according to the instructions. I am leaving now."

Your body may still feel doubtful. Done is a behavioral decision, not a feeling.

How OCD Uses Parenting Standards

New parents receive a large number of rules. Some are medical recommendations. Some are family traditions. Some are social-media opinions presented with the force of law. Some contradict one another.

OCD likes ambiguity because ambiguity creates room for another check.

If a recommendation says "avoid overheating," OCD may ask for a perfect temperature at every moment. If guidance says supervise a baby in water, OCD may demand that you never look away for a fraction of a second, then punish you for remembering a moment when you reached for a towel. If safe preparation requires clean hands, OCD may replace "clean" with a private standard that takes ten washes.

The answer is not to ignore infant-safety guidance. It is to define the real rule from a reliable source, follow it, and resist the extra ritual that exists to produce certainty.

When you are unsure what ordinary safety requires, ask a pediatric or medical professional once. Write the answer down. If you find yourself asking the same question repeatedly despite no change in circumstances, bring that pattern to your OCD clinician.

The Diagnostic Question

It is tempting to use a chapter like this as a checklist that delivers a diagnosis.

Do I have enough compulsions?

How many hours count?

What if my avoidance is not severe enough?

What if I can still work?

A formal diagnosis requires a qualified clinician. OCD is assessed through the nature of obsessions and compulsions, distress, time, impairment, insight, and differential diagnosis. The perinatal context also requires attention to mood disorders, psychosis, trauma-related symptoms, medical factors, and other conditions (Hudepohl et al., 2022; Mulcahy et al., 2023).

Self-recognition can still be useful.

You can say, "I see a recurring loop of unwanted harm thoughts followed by checking and reassurance, and it is interfering with infant care. I want an assessment for OCD."

That is a clear reason to seek help without pretending you have completed the assessment yourself.

One Compulsion, Seen Clearly

Choose one behavior or mental act that occurs often.

Do not choose the most terrifying trigger. Choose something you can observe.

Write four short lines:

Obsession: "What if I contaminated the bottle?"

Distress: "I feel uncertain and responsible."

Compulsion: "I wash it again and ask my partner."

Relief: "I feel better for fifteen minutes, then doubt the washing."

Now add a fifth line:

Possible response prevention: "Follow the ordinary cleaning step once and do not repeat it solely because the anxiety remains."

If that practice feels too difficult, make it smaller. Delay the repeat wash by two minutes. Ask one fewer reassurance question. Notice one round of mental review and stop before the next.

The aim is not to win a contest with anxiety. It is to interrupt the training cycle.

What If I Feel Worse When I Stop?

You might.

Compulsions reduce distress in the short term. If you stop using them, uncertainty can feel louder before it feels less controlling. ERP is built around approaching feared cues or uncertainty while reducing compulsive responses, usually through a planned hierarchy with a trained therapist (International OCD Foundation, n.d.).

This is why response prevention is not "force yourself through the worst thing immediately."

A good ERP plan is collaborative and graded. It considers genuine safety, readiness, severity, depression, medical issues, and the perinatal context. The book's micro-practices are designed to illustrate principles, not prescribe an individual treatment plan.

If reducing a compulsion causes overwhelming distress, major loss of function, or safety concerns, tell your clinician. Difficulty is information, not failure.

In a Nutshell

OCD is easier to recognize when you stop staring only at the thought and look at the loop around it.

The obsession creates distress or uncertainty. The compulsion tries to settle that distress. Relief arrives, but the relief is temporary. The next obsession now has evidence that a special response was required.

Compulsions can be visible or mental. Reassurance, confession, emotional checking, memory review, internet searching, and avoidance can all serve the same function as a repeated physical check.

Ordinary parenting safety has stopping rules based on proportionate guidance. OCD safety rules keep changing because their stopping rule is a feeling of certainty.

Your first useful map is not a list of every thought you have had. It is one repeated sequence you can observe. Once the cycle is visible, treatment has somewhere to begin.

Chapter 3: OCD Is Not Psychosis

The most frightening search a parent may type is not "Do I have OCD?"

It is "What if this is postpartum psychosis?"

The fear makes sense. Both OCD and postpartum psychosis can involve content about a baby being harmed. The overlap in subject matter can make two very different clinical processes look similar when reduced to a single sentence.

That is why a single sentence is not enough.

A qualified clinician does not ask only, "Did a harm thought occur?" Assessment looks at how the thought is experienced, whether the person recognizes it as coming from her own mind, whether she believes unusual ideas are literally true, whether there are hallucinations, whether mood and behavior have changed markedly, whether there is intent or a plan, how rapidly symptoms appeared, how the person is functioning, and whether safety can be maintained.

This chapter gives you language for that distinction. It cannot perform the assessment.

Why Content Cannot Decide the Diagnosis

Imagine two parents who both use the sentence, "I thought the baby was in danger because of me."

For Elena, the thought is an unwanted image. She knows it is generated by her own mind. She hates it, doubts what it says about her, and performs repeated checks to prove she would not act. She knows the feared interpretation may be irrational, but the uncertainty feels unbearable.

For another parent, the statement could occur in a very different mental state. She might hold a fixed belief that an outside force has given her a special mission involving the baby. She may hear a voice that seems external. She may be severely confused, sleeping very little without feeling tired, behaving in a markedly unusual way, or unable to question beliefs that others tell her are untrue.

The sentence about danger is similar. The clinical picture is not.

Hudak and Wisner identified insight into the obsessional nature of the thoughts as an important feature in differentiating postpartum OCD from psychosis (Hudak & Wisner, 2012). More recent reviews likewise distinguish ego-dystonic, unwanted infant-harm obsessions from psychotic experiences in which delusional beliefs or hallucinations may be present (Toor et al., 2024; Hudepohl et al., 2022).

The word *ego-dystonic* means that an experience feels inconsistent with a person's values, wishes, or sense of self. It is useful clinical language, but it is not a home safety test. Someone can be distressed for many reasons, and people can have more than one condition at the same time.

The safe conclusion is not, "If I hate the thought, I am definitely fine."

The safe conclusion is, "The way I experience the thought is one part of a full assessment."

Reality Testing

Reality testing is the capacity to distinguish internal experiences from external reality and to question beliefs that may not be true.

A person with an OCD obsession may say, "I know this sounds irrational, but I cannot stop wondering whether the thought means I will do it."

A person experiencing psychosis may be convinced of a belief that other people do not share, even when evidence is offered against it. Psychosis can also involve hallucinations, such as hearing voices or seeing things that are not present. Postpartum psychosis often includes prominent mood symptoms, and it can involve mania, depression, rapid changes in mental state, confusion, delusions, or hallucinations (Royal College of Psychiatrists, n.d.; Toor et al., 2024).

Again, real presentations are not always tidy. Insight can vary in OCD. Severe anxiety can make a person feel detached or frightened by her own mental state. Sleep deprivation can make thinking harder. Depression can coexist with OCD. A clinician may need time and collateral information from a partner or family member to understand what is happening.

If you are trying to use one feature to prove the answer to yourself, tell the clinician that too.

The Timing of Postpartum Psychosis

Postpartum psychosis is uncommon, but its seriousness changes what should happen when symptoms suggest it. NICE describes it as a severe illness that can become very severe quickly. The guideline advises immediate specialist assessment, within four hours of referral, for sudden symptoms suggesting postpartum psychosis (NICE, 2014/2020). The Royal College of Psychiatrists states that postpartum psychosis typically begins within days or weeks of childbirth and needs urgent treatment (Royal College of Psychiatrists, n.d.). Toor and colleagues describe it as a psychiatric emergency (Toor et al., 2024).

That means this is not a problem to monitor privately for several days if clear psychotic or manic symptoms are emerging.

Seek urgent medical assessment if you are experiencing hallucinations, delusions or fixed beliefs that others say are not true, severe confusion, markedly elevated or agitated mood with major behavioral change, a felt command to harm, an intention or plan to harm yourself or your baby, or an inability to keep yourself or your baby safe.

If another adult notices an abrupt and serious change in you and is concerned about psychosis, treat that concern as information worth urgent assessment rather than as an argument you must win.

Sleep: Important, but Not a Diagnostic Shortcut

Sleep is a difficult subject for new parents because nearly every parent is sleeping differently after a birth.

Ordinary infant-driven sleep disruption can leave you exhausted, foggy, irritable, and emotionally thin. That alone does not equal postpartum psychosis.

What clinicians pay attention to is the broader pattern. A person in a manic or psychotic state may need very little sleep or be unable to sleep despite the opportunity, while also showing unusual energy, agitation, pressured behavior, confusion, rapidly shifting mood, grandiose ideas, or psychotic symptoms. The combination matters more than a single bad night.

If you have been unable to sleep at all despite having the opportunity, especially with escalating mood or reality-testing changes, seek prompt medical assessment. If you are simply awake because a newborn is feeding frequently and you feel desperately tired, that is a different description, though severe sleep deprivation still deserves practical and medical support.

Do not diagnose yourself by counting hours alone.

Intent, Plan, and the Fear of Intent

Rachel's obsession was, "What if I suddenly want to hurt the baby?"

Then she checked whether she wanted to.

She imagined the feared situation and inspected her reaction. She asked herself whether an actual dangerous person would be this scared. She reviewed every moment of irritation. Soon she was not only afraid of harm. She was afraid of the possibility that an intention could appear.

An obsession about intent is not the same thing as intent.

At the same time, a book cannot infer your actual intent from the fact that you are reading it.

When clinicians assess harm risk, they may ask directly about thoughts, plans, intentions, past behavior, access to means, psychotic symptoms, mood, supports, and ability to care safely. Current Royal College of Psychiatrists standards for community perinatal mental health services explicitly include assessment of disclosures of harmful acts, delusions or hallucinations involving the infant, and thoughts, plans, or intentions of harming the infant. The guidance also tells assessors to consider that such phenomena may be intrusive obsessional thoughts (Royal College of Psychiatrists, 2026).

That is the balance this book uses.

The thought deserves to be heard.

The thought's content is not, by itself, the risk conclusion.

"But What If I Am the Exception?"

If you have OCD, the mind may use every distinction in this chapter to create a new examination.

Do I have enough insight?

What if my belief feels 49 percent real instead of 48 percent?

Was that sound outside my head or inside it?

What if I secretly have a plan but am hiding it from myself?

What if my doctor misses something?

Those questions can become compulsive.

A diagnostic distinction is meant to support appropriate assessment and treatment. It is not meant to give you a hundred-item self-test that produces permanent certainty.

If you are uncertain whether a symptom could be psychotic, tell a clinician exactly what you experienced. You can say, "I am not sure how to classify this. I want you to assess it rather than having me decide."

That is a responsible use of uncertainty.

What Hallucinations and Delusions Mean in This Context

People sometimes use *hallucination* casually to describe a vivid image in the mind. Clinically, the term usually refers to a perception-like experience occurring without a corresponding external stimulus, such as hearing a voice that seems to come from outside oneself.

A mental image that you recognize as an image in your mind is not automatically a hallucination.

A *delusion* is not simply a fear that feels intense. It is a fixed false belief held with a level of conviction that is not explained by ordinary cultural or religious context. In postpartum psychosis, delusions can involve the baby, the self, persecution, special identity, or other themes (Toor et al., 2024).

OCD can also involve poor insight, which is one reason a clinician should not use simplistic rules. The DSM diagnostic system recognizes that OCD insight can vary. A person may understand clearly that the obsessional belief is probably untrue, may be unsure, or may be highly convinced (American Psychiatric Association, 2022).

If the line feels blurry in your own case, that is an argument for assessment, not for hiding the symptom.

Mania and Severe Mood Change

Postpartum psychosis is often associated with bipolar-spectrum illness, and mania or severe mood symptoms may be part of the presentation (Toor et al., 2024; NICE, 2014/2020).

Mania is more than having a productive day or feeling keyed up because you are anxious. It can involve markedly elevated or irritable mood, unusually increased energy or activity, reduced need for sleep, rapid speech, racing thoughts, impulsive or risky behavior, inflated self-importance, and impaired judgment. In a postpartum emergency, these changes may occur alongside psychotic symptoms or severe confusion.

A frightened person with OCD can read that list and start checking every ordinary variation. "I talked fast to my sister. Was that mania?" "I ordered baby clothes online. Was that impulsive?" This is why lists need context.

Clinicians assess degree, change from baseline, clustering of symptoms, duration, impairment, and the whole mental state.

If people close to you are reporting a marked change and you are in the early postpartum period, or if you recognize several severe symptoms occurring together, seek medical assessment promptly.

When OCD and Other Conditions Coexist

OCD does not create a protective bubble around other mental health problems.

A person can have OCD and depression. A person with bipolar disorder can also have obsessive-compulsive symptoms. Trauma symptoms, panic, generalized anxiety, eating disorders, substance use, medical illness, or medication effects can complicate the picture. Perinatal assessment therefore needs more than an OCD checklist (Mulcahy et al., 2023; Hudepohl et al., 2022).

This matters for readers who have found a perfect match with an OCD description online and are tempted to stop there.

Recognition is useful. Assessment is broader.

If you have a personal history of bipolar disorder, psychosis, or severe perinatal mental illness, or a close family history that increases concern, tell your maternity and mental health clinicians. NICE recommends particular vigilance for postpartum psychosis in people with a history of severe mental illness or a first-degree family history of severe perinatal mental illness (NICE, 2014/2020).

That is not a prediction that you will become ill. It is information that can shape monitoring and care planning.

A Phone Note for Urgent Signs

Do this exercise when you are relatively calm, not while conducting a frantic symptom search.

Create a note titled **Urgent Assessment**.

Write:

"I will seek urgent medical assessment if I have hallucinations, fixed beliefs that others say are not true, severe confusion, major manic or behavioral change, a felt command to harm, actual intent or a plan to harm myself or my baby, or I cannot maintain safety."

Then add the local route you would use.

In the United States, that may include calling 911 for an immediate emergency, going to the nearest emergency department, or calling or texting 988 for crisis support when appropriate. In the United Kingdom, NHS 111 can advise on urgent care and 999 is for emergencies. Elsewhere, write your local emergency number and urgent mental health service if you know it.

The purpose is to reduce decision-making during a crisis. It is not a list to reread every hour to prove you do not meet the criteria.

Two Different Clinical Questions

OCD asks: "Can I be completely certain that I am not dangerous?"

Risk assessment asks: "Given the full current picture, what level of care and protection is appropriate now?"

Those are different questions.

The first has no permanent answer that OCD will accept.

The second can be addressed with evidence, clinical judgment, observation, history, and a plan.

This is why telling the truth to a clinician matters more than producing the perfect self-diagnosis. You do not have to arrive at the appointment already knowing whether every experience is an obsession, a panic symptom, a depressive thought, a trauma reaction, a medication effect, or something else.

Your task is description.
Their task is assessment.

Principles to Remember

Infant-harm content can occur in both OCD and psychosis, so content alone does not determine diagnosis or risk. Clinicians look at reality testing, insight, intent, planning, mood, behavior, sleep, function, history, and other symptoms.

Postpartum psychosis is uncommon but serious. Sudden psychotic or manic symptoms after birth need urgent medical assessment, and clear intent or inability to maintain safety is an emergency regardless of diagnostic label.

Distress about a thought can fit an ego-dystonic obsession, but distress is not a guarantee. Likewise, a vivid mental image that you recognize as internal is not automatically a hallucination.

If you are uncertain how to classify a symptom, describe it without editing and ask a qualified clinician to assess it. The responsible goal is not to prove a diagnosis at home. It is to get the right level of care for the real presentation.

Chapter 4: Why the Alarm Chooses What Matters

Sofia did not have a harm obsession about every person she passed.

The thought attached to her baby.

That fact felt significant to her. If the subject mattered this much, surely the thought must reveal something deep. She spent days asking why her mind had selected the person she loved most.

The answer she wanted was a biography of the thought. If she could trace it to the right source, she believed she could close the case.

OCD offered unlimited theories.

Maybe she was resentful about sleep.

Maybe birth had changed her.

Maybe an argument with her own mother had awakened something.

Maybe she had never really known herself.

The search for an origin became another way to avoid the simpler problem: she could not tolerate leaving the thought unexplained.

Importance Creates Sensitivity

Imagine two bowls on a table. One contains spare buttons. The other contains medication for your baby.

You will pay more attention to the second bowl.

That does not mean attention caused the medication to become dangerous. It means importance changes how closely you monitor possible mistakes.

Parenthood creates many high-importance domains at once: feeding, sleep, health, hygiene, transport, attachment, development, and physical safety. The cost of a mistake can feel enormous. For someone prone to OCD, this high responsibility can become a setting in which uncertainty is treated as unacceptable.

Perinatal OCD literature repeatedly describes heightened responsibility for infant safety and obsessions centered on harm, contamination, and mistakes (Hudepohl et al., 2022; Royal College of Psychiatrists, n.d.).

You do not need a romantic explanation such as "only the most loving parents get these thoughts." That claim goes too far. Loving a baby does not diagnose OCD, and people with serious mental illness also love their children.

A more careful statement is enough: OCD often attaches to personally important areas where uncertainty and responsibility already matter.

Responsibility Can Quietly Become Omnipotence

Amara's rule was, "If something bad happens and I could have prevented it, it is my fault."

At first, that sounded like conscientious parenting.

Then the word *could* expanded.

Could she have checked the bottle one more time?

Could she have stayed awake while the baby slept?

Could she have researched a rare condition?

Could she have avoided a stroller route where a freak accident was imaginable?

If prevention is possible in theory, responsibility becomes infinite.

Ordinary responsibility asks what a reasonable person can know and do with the information available. Inflated responsibility acts as if you must anticipate every possible path to harm and close it.

That standard is impossible. It is also seductive because every extra precaution feels morally serious.

The way out is not carelessness. It is proportion.

What would count as ordinary care if you were not trying to eliminate every imagined possibility?

That question can be hard to answer alone when OCD has been setting the rules for weeks. A pediatrician can clarify infant-care guidance. An OCD-trained therapist can help identify which additions function as compulsions.

The Impossible Standard of the Perfect Mother

There is a cultural layer too.

Parents, and mothers in particular, are often exposed to strong messages that a good parent anticipates needs, remains patient, feels grateful, bonds naturally, protects constantly, and makes informed choices. Online parenting spaces can turn ordinary preferences into moral categories.

OCD can take these standards literally.

If a good mother protects, then more protection must be better.

If a good mother enjoys closeness, then boredom must be suspicious.

If a good mother does not want harm, then an unwanted harm image must require explanation.

The problem is not that standards exist. Babies depend on adults. Care has real duties.

The problem is the conversion of a reasonable value into a demand for perfect internal and external control.

You can be responsible without being omniscient.

You can love without feeling love every second.

You can protect without preventing every possible accident.

You can have an unwanted thought without holding a tribunal about what kind of mother would have it.

Why "Why?" Can Become a Compulsion

Questions are not compulsions by definition.

If a clinician asks when symptoms began, that history matters. If you notice that OCD worsened after a severe sleep disruption, that may help treatment planning. If a medication change coincided with new symptoms, a prescriber needs that information.

The compulsive version of *why* has a different structure.

It repeats after reasonable answers have been found.

It demands a morally satisfying explanation.

It treats uncertainty about origin as evidence of danger.

It keeps you from moving to the next useful action.

Suppose you learn that intrusive harm thoughts are described in perinatal OCD. The mind says, "Fine, but why did *my* exact image involve that exact object on that exact day?"

There may be no answer worth having.

Brains combine recent cues, fears, memories, sensations, and random associations. A thought can be triggered by something obvious or by nothing you can identify. The treatment plan does not depend on solving the genealogy of every image.

A useful boundary is: "I will gather history for assessment, but I will not investigate every thought as if it contains a hidden message."

Uncertainty Is Built Into Infant Care

Tessa wanted a rule for everything.

How warm should the room be?

How long could the baby cry before it caused damage?

Was this rash normal?

Was that amount of spit-up normal?

Could the carrier cause harm if one strap looked slightly uneven?

Some questions had clear medical answers. Some depended on context. Some could not be answered with certainty.

That last category was unbearable.

OCD can make uncertainty itself feel like negligence. If you are unsure, the mind says you have not done enough.

But uncertainty is not the same as inaction.

A parent can follow current medical guidance, call a clinician when a symptom meets a threshold, use ordinary safety equipment correctly, and still live with residual uncertainty. There is no version of parenting in which every future outcome is known.

ERP uses this fact rather than fighting it. Exposure is not only contact with a feared object. It can be contact with uncertainty. Response prevention means not performing the ritual designed to make that uncertainty disappear (International OCD Foundation, n.d.).

What Perfectionism Adds

Perfectionism can interact with OCD when mistakes are treated as unacceptable or as proof of personal failure. Perinatal research has examined perfectionism and responsibility-related beliefs among factors associated with obsessive-compulsive symptoms, though no single personality trait explains the disorder (Hudepohl et al., 2022).

The distinction matters because a reader may hear "perfectionism" and blame herself.

OCD is not a punishment for being organized.

Nor is recovery a command to become sloppy.

The practical issue is what happens after an ordinary imperfection. If you misread a label and correct it, can the mistake end? Or do you replay it for two hours to determine whether a careful mother would have made it?

A flexible standard allows correction.

A compulsive standard demands retroactive certainty.

The Meaning of Anger

One common trap is the combination of an intrusive thought and a normal moment of anger.

The baby has been crying for a long time. You feel frustrated. Then a harm image appears.

The mind joins the two events.

"There. That proves it. The thought came when I was angry."

Parents can feel anger, irritation, resentment, boredom, and the wish for a break. Those emotions do not automatically equal intent. At the same time, intense anger plus concern that you may lose control deserves practical safety planning and support.

If you are overwhelmed, put the baby in a safe place according to standard infant-care guidance and step away briefly if needed, or hand care to another safe adult. If you fear you may act violently, seek immediate help.

For OCD, the work is different when there is no intent and the problem is an obsessional interpretation. You do not need to prove you were zero percent angry. You need to stop using the emotion as forensic evidence.

"Protective Parents Get Violent Thoughts" Needs Careful Language

You may have seen social-media posts saying that violent intrusive thoughts happen *because* you are a loving or protective parent.

There is a useful idea inside that statement and a risk of overstatement.

The useful idea is that obsessional themes often involve things a person cares about deeply. That helps explain why the content feels so potent.

The overstatement is turning love into a diagnostic guarantee.

Someone can be distressed by a thought and still need a full assessment. Someone can love a baby and experience psychosis, depression, mania, substance-related symptoms, or another condition. Someone can have OCD without being able to articulate a tender emotional response in the moment.

So this book will not ask you to prove safety by proving love.

It will ask you to describe symptoms accurately and direct your behavior according to values, real safety, and appropriate professional care.

That is less comforting for five minutes and more reliable over time.

The Salience Loop

Attention changes what you notice.

Suppose you decide that a particular intrusive image is the most dangerous thing your mind can produce. You monitor for it. Each appearance triggers analysis. Each analysis makes the image memorable. Each memory raises the chance you will notice it again.

Soon the image seems unusually frequent.

Frequency can then become evidence: "If it appears this much, it must matter."

This creates a salience loop.

You do not have to decide whether the thought appeared because it mattered or mattered because you watched for it. You can stop feeding the loop at the response stage.

The next time it appears, note it once and return attention outward.

What color is the baby's sock you are putting on?

What sentence is your partner saying?

What is the next line on the grocery list?

This is not distraction used to force the thought away. The thought is allowed to remain in the background. You are choosing where to put behavior.

Values Without Self-Testing

Values can be useful in recovery because they answer, "What do I want to do?" rather than "How do I want to feel?"

If caregiving matters to you, a values-based action might be completing the diaper change despite an intrusive image.

If honesty matters, it might be telling your clinician the content you have been editing out.

If partnership matters, it might be asking for a planned hour of rest without making your partner reassure you first.

The trap is turning values into another purity test.

"Did I do that lovingly enough?"

"Was I truly present?"

"Did I enjoy it the right amount?"

Values are directions for action, not scores for internal experience.

You can choose a caring action while anxious, irritated, numb, or uncertain.

An Exercise: The Responsibility Sentence

Write one sentence that begins:

"The responsibility I am trying to make 100 percent certain is..."

Examples:

"...that I can prevent every accident."

"...that I will never feel angry while holding my baby."

"...that I will always know whether a thought is harmless."

"...that no clinician could ever misunderstand me."

Read your sentence once.

Then write:

"A reasonable responsibility I can actually carry is..."

Examples:

"...following ordinary safety guidance and asking for help when something changes."

"...putting the baby down safely and taking a break if I am overwhelmed."

"...describing the thought and my response to a qualified clinician."

"...preparing a clear disclosure rather than trying to control another person's reaction."

The exercise is not about lowering care. It is about replacing infinite responsibility with a task that can be completed.

When Uncertainty Feels Like a Moral Failure

For some readers, "allow uncertainty" sounds irresponsible.

If the feared topic were unimportant, perhaps uncertainty would be tolerable. But this is your baby.

That is exactly why the work is hard.

You do not practice uncertainty about whether to use a car seat. You use the car seat.

You practice uncertainty about the extra question OCD adds after you have followed the real rule.

"Did I fasten it exactly right even though I checked according to the instructions?"

"Could there be a hidden defect nobody knows about?"

"What if my brief frustration means something terrible?"

Ordinary safety handles the actionable risk.

OCD asks for a second layer that can never be complete.

Learning to separate those layers is not a retreat from responsibility. It is a way to spend your attention on responsibilities that can actually be carried.

When Responsibility Becomes a Feeling

One more trap deserves a name. Responsibility can become something you try to *feel* before you stop.

You follow the actual rule, but you still feel careless. So you add a check. The check does not change the facts. It changes the feeling for a moment.

This is how a practical duty can turn into an emotional requirement.

Try separating the two statements:

"I completed the safety task."

"I feel completely certain that I completed it."

Only the first can usually be finished through behavior. The second may remain unsettled.

When the feeling lags behind the facts, practice ending the task anyway. If you genuinely discover new evidence, respond to it. If the only new evidence is lingering anxiety, let the feeling catch up on its own schedule.

This is a small rehearsal for later ERP. You are teaching the mind that responsibility can end before certainty arrives.

One More Responsibility Practice

Pick one rule that begins with "I must make sure."

Rewrite it with a stopping point.

"I must make sure the baby is safe" is too large.

"I will follow the pediatric sleep guidance, respond to new symptoms, and ask for medical advice when the agreed threshold is met" can be completed.

The first rule makes you responsible for the future. The second makes you responsible for behavior available now.

Use the same rewrite for one other area this week. If the new sentence still requires a feeling such as "until I am sure," it does not yet have a stopping point.

In a Nutshell

OCD often attaches to important areas because importance increases attention, responsibility, and the wish for certainty. Parenthood supplies all three.

That does not justify the slogan that only loving parents get violent thoughts. Love is not a diagnostic test. The useful point is narrower: obsessional themes often target what feels morally or practically important.

Inflated responsibility turns "do what a reasonable parent can do" into "prevent every imaginable bad outcome." Perfectionism can then make ordinary mistakes feel like evidence.

The question *why* can help with clinical history, but it can also become rumination when it demands a complete explanation for every thought.

Recovery asks you to carry reasonable responsibility while leaving some uncertainty unresolved. That is the foundation for the response-prevention work ahead.

Chapter 5: The Compulsions That Keep It Loud

Mei could tell you exactly how many times she had checked the front door. She could not tell you how many times she had checked her own mind.

That work happened while she fed the baby, pushed the stroller, showered, and tried to watch television with her partner. She replayed the same image. She measured her disgust. She reconstructed the seconds before it appeared. She asked whether a dangerous person would be doing so much checking.

By the end of the day, the original thought had occupied less time than the investigation.

A compulsion is not defined by what it looks like. It is defined partly by what it is trying to do. If an act is repeatedly used to lower obsessional distress, prevent a feared event, or obtain certainty, it can become part of the OCD cycle. Perinatal OCD can include both visible rituals and private mental acts (Hudepohl et al., 2022; Royal College of Psychiatrists, n.d.).

The private ones are often the last to be recognized.

Rumination Is Work

Rumination can feel passive because you are "just thinking." In practice, it is effort.

You pose a question.

You search memory.

You compare interpretations.

You reject an answer.

You reopen the question.

The subject may be moral: "What kind of person would have that thought?"

It may be predictive: "What if I lose control?"

It may be diagnostic: "Was that an obsession or an urge?"

It may be emotional: "Did I feel enough love?"

The shared feature is the demand for resolution.

Rumination differs from ordinary reflection in its stopping rule. Reflection can end with a decision, an accepted limit, or the recognition that more information is needed from someone qualified. Rumination keeps going because certainty has not arrived.

Try this test: if you have asked the same core question five times and no new external information is available, the next round is unlikely to be a better investigation.

That is a point at which response prevention can begin.

Memory Review

A harm obsession often sends the mind backward.

You remember an argument from ten years ago.

You remember snapping at a pet.

You remember a childhood game with a violent theme.

You remember enjoying a crime novel.

Each memory is brought into the present as evidence.

The mind says, "If you are going to trust yourself with a baby, you should check your entire history."

There is no entire history available for inspection. Memory is incomplete. Context changes. Ordinary human behavior contains contradictions. The more you review, the more uncertain small details can feel.

Memory review can therefore become self-defeating. The goal is perfect confidence in your character, but the method creates more material to doubt.

A response-prevention phrase might be: "I am not reviewing old evidence for this question."

Then redirect to a current task.

The goal is not to replace a negative memory with a positive one. That would keep the trial open.

Checking Your Body

Some parents monitor bodily sensations after an intrusive thought.

Did my heart speed up because I was scared or excited?

Why did my hand feel tense?

Did I have a sexual sensation during diapering?

Why do I feel numb?

Bodies produce sensations for many reasons. Attention itself changes what you notice. Anxiety can heighten arousal. Fatigue can flatten emotion. Hormonal changes, pain, feeding, medication, and ordinary physiology can add noise.

OCD turns the noise into a test.

This can be especially distressing with sexual-harm obsessions. A person may inspect genital sensation or emotional reaction to determine whether an unwanted thought reveals attraction. Repeated checking keeps attention fixed on the feared signal and can make ambiguous sensations feel more important.

Do not use a body scan as a lie detector.

If you have a real medical symptom, discuss it with a medical professional. If the behavior is repeated monitoring designed to settle a moral question, treat the monitoring as part of the OCD cycle.

Reassurance From People

Tessa had a reliable question: "Do you think I am safe with the baby?"

Her partner had a reliable answer: "Of course."

For three weeks, that exchange happened several times a day.

It looked like support. It functioned like a ritual.

Reassurance is tricky because people need connection. A frightened parent should be able to say she is struggling. A partner should be able to respond with care. The problem begins when the response must contain certainty and must be repeated whenever doubt returns.

Support can address the distress without answering the obsession.

"I know this is hard. What does your treatment plan say to do when the question comes back?"

"I can stay with you while you let the uncertainty be here."

"Do you need practical help, or are you asking me to settle the OCD question?"

Those responses may feel less soothing at first. They also stop making the partner responsible for producing a feeling that cannot last.

Reassurance From Professionals

Clinicians can be pulled into reassurance loops too.

A parent asks, "Are you sure this is OCD?"

The clinician explains the formulation.

The parent returns: "But what about the fact that the image felt vivid?"

The clinician explains again.

Then the parent asks whether the clinician has ever seen that exact image.

Good care includes psychoeducation and honest discussion of risk. But repeated certainty-giving can become unhelpful when the question has already been assessed and no new information is present.

If you notice this pattern, say it directly: "I think I am using appointments to get reassurance. Can we agree on what information should trigger a new risk discussion and what should be handled as an OCD question?"

That creates a boundary between responsible reassessment and compulsive repetition.

Internet Searching

The internet is useful for finding a qualified therapist, reading a treatment guideline, checking a medication information source with your prescriber, or learning the basics of OCD.

It is also an infinite reassurance machine.

A compulsive search often has recognizable features. You use the same phrases. You search until you find a particular conclusion. You skip pages that increase anxiety. You compare yourself with strangers. You return despite having learned nothing new.

The relief is brief.

Set a purpose before you search.

"I need three OCD therapists who offer ERP."

"I need the official phone number for the perinatal service."

"I need the patient information page my prescriber told me to read."

When the task is complete, close the search.

If your purpose is "I need to find one more story proving someone had my exact thought and did not act," the search is serving the obsession.

Confessing Every Variation

Nia told her sister about a violent image. Her sister responded calmly.

An hour later Nia returned.

"I left out that I was annoyed right before it happened."

Her sister reassured her.

Then Nia remembered that she had been standing close to the baby.

Another confession.

Confession can temporarily reduce guilt. That relief can teach the mind that every variation must be disclosed to remain morally safe.

A useful distinction is between **clinically relevant disclosure** and **compulsive completeness**.

A clinician needs enough information to assess the thought, your relationship to it, intent, planning, psychotic symptoms, compulsions, impairment, and other relevant factors. If new information changes risk, you should share it.

Compulsive completeness demands a transcript of every mental event so another person can absolve you.

You can ask your clinician to help define the line.

Avoidance

Avoidance may be the most costly compulsion because it can shrink a parent's role.

First you stop one task.

Then you stop being alone with the baby.

Then you avoid a room associated with the thought.

Then you avoid friends who talk about difficult parenting moments because their stories trigger images.

Your world becomes organized around preventing internal discomfort.

ERP treatment generally works in the opposite direction: approach feared situations or thoughts in a graded, planned way and reduce the compulsive response (International OCD Foundation, n.d.).

That does not mean you should remove every safety measure or force yourself into a situation you cannot manage. Real risks and medical limitations still count. A therapist can help distinguish ordinary safety from avoidance whose main function is anxiety reduction.

The aim is to reclaim ordinary life, not perform dramatic bravery.

Delegation Can Be Practical or Compulsive

New parents should share work when possible.

Handing the baby to a partner because you need sleep, pain limits movement, or you both planned to divide feeds is ordinary cooperation.

Handing over every diaper change because an unwanted sexual thought appeared may be avoidance.

The action looks identical. The function differs.

Ask: "If the intrusive thought were not present, would I make the same choice for the same practical reason?"

If yes, the decision may simply be good household management.

If no, and the main reason is "I need to eliminate the chance that the thought could mean something," discuss that avoidance with an OCD-trained clinician.

This question is not perfect. It is a way to begin seeing the pattern.

Self-Reassurance

You can perform reassurance without another person.

"I am a good mom."

"I would never do that."

"People with OCD do not act on thoughts."

"My therapist said I am safe."

These statements may all contain information you believe. Repeating them to neutralize each obsession can still function as a compulsion.

Response prevention does not require replacing them with frightening statements. You do not need to say, "Maybe I will definitely do it," which is logically confused.

You can use uncertainty language:

"I notice I want a guarantee."

"I am not answering that question again."

"I can follow the plan without feeling certain."

Then return to behavior.

Testing

Testing tries to manufacture proof.

You hold the baby while imagining harm and inspect whether you move.

You stand near a household object and check whether an urge appears.

You look at a photograph and grade your emotional response.

You deliberately provoke the thought without a treatment plan, not to practice uncertainty, but to see whether you pass.

Testing is not the same as ERP.

ERP has a therapeutic purpose, a planned target, and response prevention. It is not an examination of whether you are a good person. When exposures are used as tests, every ambiguous reaction becomes a reason to repeat them.

Chapter 10 will show how to build a small ERP ladder without turning it into a private courtroom.

Delay Before Drop

If stopping a compulsion feels impossible, use delay.

When you want to search, wait two minutes.

When you want to ask for reassurance, write the question down and wait five.

When you begin mental review, notice the first round and decline the second.

Delay teaches you that the urge to ritualize can be present without dictating immediate behavior.

Over time, the goal is not permanent postponement. It is less obedience to the compulsion.

A short delay is especially useful during newborn care because it does not require a special setting. You can practice while warming a bottle, folding clothes, or waiting for a partner to finish a task.

Track Behavior, Not Horror

If you keep notes, do not create a catalog of every intrusive image.

That can increase monitoring.

Track the behavior you want to change.

"Asked partner for certainty four times."

"Re-read symptom page twice."

"Avoided bath time."

"Spent thirty minutes reviewing memory."

Then choose one target.

"Tomorrow I will ask one fewer reassurance question."

"Tomorrow I will do the ordinary diaper change and not check my feelings afterward."

Data should guide practice, not build a case against you.

The Compulsion After the Compulsion

OCD can add a second ritual after you notice the first.

You ask for reassurance, then realize reassurance may be a compulsion. Now you review whether asking was "bad for recovery." You search whether one reassurance question can undo ERP. You ask your therapist to certify that you did not ruin treatment.

The subject changed from safety to recovery. The function stayed the same.

This is worth noticing because people who learn OCD terminology can become highly skilled at checking themselves with clinical language.

Did I ruminate?

Was that avoidance?

Did I allow uncertainty correctly?

Did I accidentally self-reassure?

Treatment needs reflection, but it does not need constant self-surveillance.

A workable stopping rule is to review practice at a scheduled time, often with your therapist, rather than after every mental event. If you spot a clear ritual in real time, redirect. If you are unsure, make a brief note and keep moving.

When a Compulsion Is Also a Habit

Some behaviors begin as anxiety reduction and then become routine.

You may reach for the phone before you consciously notice fear. You may ask your partner a familiar question while thinking about something else. The ritual has been repeated enough that the sequence starts quickly.

That does not make response prevention impossible.

Add a physical pause.

Put the phone in another room during one predictable trigger.

Write a small card near the monitor: "What is the real task?"

Ask your partner to respond to the first familiar reassurance question with, "Is this the question we are reducing?"

The cue is not meant to become another ritual. It creates just enough space for choice.

Over time, the goal is to need fewer cues because the new response has become familiar too.

The Cost Question

A compulsion often advertises only its benefit.

"It makes me feel safer."

Ask for the full price.

How much time does it take?

What task does it replace?

Who else has to participate?

What happens when you cannot perform it?

Does the rule grow?

A check that takes thirty seconds may seem cheap until it is repeated forty times and determines whether you can leave the house.

Write the cost of one ritual in ordinary terms: minutes, missed activities, transferred care, arguments, lost sleep, or attention taken from the baby.

This is not meant to shame you. It gives treatment a concrete reason to change the behavior beyond the abstract goal of "having less OCD."

Principles to Remember

Compulsions are attempts to reduce distress, prevent a feared event, or obtain certainty. They can be visible or completely private.

Rumination, memory review, body checking, reassurance, internet searching, confession, avoidance, delegation, self-reassurance, and testing can all enter the cycle.

The question is not whether an action looks sensible. Ask what job it is doing and how long its relief lasts.

Support and information still matter. The change is to stop using them as repeated certainty rituals.

Pick one compulsion you can observe. Delay it, shorten it, or drop one repetition. Small response prevention is still response prevention.

Chapter 6: The Fear of Telling Someone

Leah had rehearsed the appointment in her car.

She planned to say, "I have postpartum anxiety."

That was true. It was also incomplete.

The part she left out was the reason she no longer prepared dinner while holding the baby in a carrier. An unwanted violent image had appeared weeks earlier. Since then, Leah had treated the kitchen as evidence. She avoided it, checked her reactions around household objects, and asked her husband to watch the baby whenever she cooked.

At the appointment, the clinician asked whether she had frightening thoughts about the baby.

Leah said, "Sometimes."

The question she most needed help with remained hidden.

Fear of disclosure is not irrational in the sense of being silly. Parents know that professionals have duties to protect children. They may have heard alarming stories online. They may not know whether a clinician understands OCD. They may fear that saying the content aloud will make it sound like intent.

This chapter cannot promise what any individual professional, health system, or child-protection agency will do. Laws, safeguarding duties, thresholds, and service structures differ by jurisdiction. It can show you how a competent assessment separates content from risk and how to provide information that makes your experience clearer.

The Myth of the Magic Sentence

There is no phrase that guarantees an outcome.

"I have intrusive thoughts" is useful language, but it does not exempt someone from assessment.

"I would never hurt my baby" may express how you feel, but a clinician still needs to understand the wider presentation.

"I think it is OCD" can help orient the conversation, but self-diagnosis does not replace evaluation.

The goal of a disclosure script is not to control the assessor. It is to prevent fear from deleting the information they need.

That is a different purpose.

What Current Perinatal Standards Ask Clinicians to Consider

Royal College of Psychiatrists standards for community perinatal mental health services provide a useful example of how professional assessment is structured. The standards say risk assessment should include harmful acts, delusions or hallucinations involving the infant, and thoughts, plans, or intentions of harming the infant. The guidance specifically tells clinicians to consider that such phenomena may be intrusive obsessional thoughts (Royal College of Psychiatrists, 2026).

That wording matters.

It does not say, "Ignore harm thoughts."

It does not say, "Treat every harm thought as intent."

It says assessment must consider the possibility that the phenomena are obsessional while still assessing risk.

This is the middle ground a frightened parent often cannot imagine.

What to Include in a Disclosure

A useful disclosure describes more than content.

You can tell the clinician:

What the thought is like: image, sentence, impulse, urge, doubt, or belief.

Whether it is wanted or unwanted.

Whether you have any intention or plan to act.

Whether you believe the thought or recognize it as coming from your own mind.

Whether you hear voices or see things other people do not.

What you do afterward: check, avoid, seek reassurance, confess, research, wash, review, or transfer care.

How much time it consumes.

How it changes infant care.

Whether you have depression, suicidal thoughts, severe agitation, unusual energy, confusion, or major sleep changes.

Whether anything has happened that created an actual safety concern.

This information gives a clinician a pattern to assess.

A Six-Sentence Script

If speaking becomes difficult, write this down before the appointment.

"I have repeated unwanted thoughts or images about harming my baby, and I am frightened by them."

"I do not want these thoughts, and I need help understanding whether they are part of OCD or another condition."

"I have been responding by ______ (checking, avoiding, asking for reassurance, reviewing, or another behavior)."

"I ______ (do or do not) have any intention or plan to act on the thoughts."

"I ______ (do or do not) have experiences such as hearing voices, fixed beliefs others say are not true, severe confusion, or unusually elevated or agitated mood."

"The symptoms are affecting me by ______ (time lost, tasks avoided, sleep affected, bonding checked, work disrupted, or another concrete impact)."

Do not copy a sentence that is untrue.

If you have intent, say that.

If you are unsure whether you have intent, say, "I am not sure how to understand this and I need you to assess it."

If you have heard a voice, do not change the wording to make it sound like an ordinary thought.

Accuracy matters more than producing an OCD-shaped story.

"Will They Take My Baby Away?"

This is often the hidden question behind disclosure.

No responsible book can answer it with a universal yes or no.

Safeguarding and child-protection systems vary. Professionals may have mandatory duties when they believe a child faces a risk of harm. Decisions depend on the actual circumstances, including current risk, behavior, intent, psychotic symptoms, the baby's care, supports, local law, and service policy.

At the same time, mental illness or the existence of an intrusive thought does not mechanically determine a child-protection outcome. Current Royal College of Psychiatrists standards require perinatal risk assessment to consider harmful acts, delusions or hallucinations, and thoughts, plans, or intentions involving the infant, while specifically noting that some phenomena may be intrusive obsessional thoughts (Royal College of Psychiatrists, 2026).

The most defensible approach is transparency about the limit: disclosure can lead to further questions, safety planning, referral, or safeguarding action when professionals judge it necessary. It can also lead to recognition of OCD and access to treatment. Nobody writing generally for an international audience can promise the path in your individual case.

If you want to understand local confidentiality and safeguarding rules, ask before or at the start of the appointment: "Can you explain your confidentiality limits and when you are required to make a safeguarding report?"

That is a normal question.

Why Hiding Can Backfire Clinically

If you say only, "I worry a lot," a clinician may reasonably explore generalized anxiety.

If the actual pattern is "I have unwanted images of intentional harm, I avoid being alone with the baby, and I spend hours checking whether I might act," the fuller description points toward a different assessment.

Perinatal OCD is at risk of being missed or misdiagnosed, which is one reason experts have developed perinatal-specific assessment and treatment recommendations (Mulcahy et al., 2023).

Hiding content can also create a strange loop. You leave the appointment without having been understood, then tell yourself, "The clinician did not say it was OCD." But the clinician never received the information needed to consider OCD properly.

Disclosure does not guarantee diagnosis. It makes a better assessment possible.

Bringing a Written Note

Samira could speak clearly about almost anything until she tried to describe the image.

She printed one page.

At the top she wrote the six-sentence script. Underneath, she listed the compulsions and how long they took. At the bottom, she wrote three questions:

"Could this be OCD?"

"How are you assessing the difference between obsession and intent or psychosis?"

"If you think I need more specialized care, where will you refer me?"

A written note can reduce the chance that shame edits the appointment.

It can also become compulsive if you rewrite it forty times to make sure every word proves innocence.

Use a stopping rule.

One page. One revision for clarity. Bring it.

Taking Someone With You

A partner or trusted person can help if they understand their role.

Their job is not to testify that you are a good person.

They can describe changes they have observed, help you remember dates, tell the clinician about sleep or functioning, take notes, and support you after the appointment.

If there are symptoms that affect insight or reality testing, collateral information can be especially useful.

Before the visit, agree that the support person will not interrupt every difficult question with reassurance. Let the clinician complete the assessment.

When a Professional Reacts Poorly

Some clinicians know OCD well. Some do not.

A professional may look surprised because the content is taboo. They may ask direct questions because risk assessment requires them. A surprised face does not automatically mean they have decided you are dangerous.

If the clinician appears to equate the presence of any intrusive harm thought with intent without exploring compulsions, insight, planning, psychotic symptoms, or context, you can ask:

"Can you explain how you are distinguishing an intrusive obsession from intent?"

"Are you familiar with perinatal OCD and harm obsessions?"

"Would it be appropriate to involve a perinatal mental health or OCD specialist?"

Do not use these questions to argue against a safety decision when there is a genuine concern. Use them to ask for a clear clinical rationale.

If you disagree with an assessment, ask what second-opinion or specialist-referral options exist in your system.

If the Clinician Asks About Suicide

Do not be offended by the question.

OCD can coexist with depression, and perinatal mental health assessments often include self-harm and suicide risk. The question is part of understanding the whole picture.

Answer accurately.

If you have intrusive self-harm obsessions but no wish to die, describe that distinction.

If you do want to die, or you have a plan, say so.

If you are unsure, say you are unsure.

The goal is not to make every answer fit OCD. It is to get the right care.

Confidentiality Has Limits

Mental health care is generally confidential, but confidentiality is not absolute. The exact rules depend on where you live, the professional's role, and the circumstances. Clinicians may need to share information when there is a serious safety concern or a legal safeguarding duty.

You can ask for the rules in plain language.

"What stays confidential?"

"What kinds of concerns require you to share information?"

"If you need to share something, will you tell me what happens next when possible?"

Those questions help turn a vague fear into specific information.

They do not change the clinician's duties.

The Appointment After the Appointment

OCD may conduct a review on the way home.

Why did the clinician pause?

Why did she write that down?

Why did he ask the question twice?

Did I sound convincing?

Should I email a clarification?

Before the appointment, plan for this.

Decide what follow-up is genuinely needed. If the clinician asks you to send a medication list or complete a form, do that. If you realize you omitted material that changes risk, share it.

If the urge is to send a fifth email explaining that your facial expression did not mean anything, wait and discuss the reassurance pattern at the next session.

The assessment itself can become a trigger. That does not make the assessment wrong.

A Disclosure Rehearsal

Read your six sentences aloud once.

Notice which sentence is hardest.

Do not practice until you sound perfectly calm. Calmness is not evidence.

Do not remove the hardest sentence because saying it increases anxiety.

If the content is too difficult to speak, hand the clinician the note.

Add one sentence about what you want from the appointment:

"I would like an assessment for perinatal OCD and any other condition that could explain these symptoms, and I want to know what treatment you recommend."

That keeps the visit centered on care rather than confession.

What If You Have Already Been Reassured by a Professional?

Sometimes the feared appointment goes well. A clinician recognizes the obsessional pattern and recommends OCD treatment.

Then the mind asks for the appointment again.

You may want another professional to confirm the same conclusion, then another. A second opinion can be appropriate when diagnosis is uncertain, treatment is not helping, risk has changed, or a specialist review is warranted. Repeated opinions whose only purpose is to make the same fear go away can become reassurance.

Ask yourself what new decision the next opinion would change.

If the answer is clear, seek it.

If the answer is "I want to hear one more person say I am not dangerous," bring that urge into OCD treatment.

If English Is Not Your First Language

Taboo thoughts are hard enough to describe in the language you use most comfortably.

If you need an interpreter, ask whether the service can provide one. Do not rely on a child or another person who should not be placed in that role.

You can write key phrases in advance.

"Unwanted thought."

"No intent."

"I am unsure."

"I hear a voice."

"I have a plan."

"I check repeatedly."

Accurate interpretation matters because small differences in wording can affect how the experience is understood.

If cultural or religious meanings are part of the fear, say so. The clinician needs to know what is ordinary in your community and what is new, unwanted, or impairing for you.

After a Safeguarding Discussion

If safeguarding is discussed, ask for concrete next steps.

What concern is being assessed?

Who will be contacted?

What information will be shared?

What happens next?

What support is available to you and the baby?

Then resist the urge to infer meaning from every administrative detail.

A referral or consultation is a process, not a verdict about your character. Cooperate with legitimate assessment, ask reasonable questions, and use your own support while the process unfolds.

If You Fear the Record Itself

Some parents worry that once an intrusive thought appears in a medical record it will follow them forever.

Health-record practices differ by system, and a book cannot tell you who can access a record in your jurisdiction. You can ask the service what is documented, who can see it, how confidentiality works, and how corrections are handled if factual errors occur.

Do not let uncertainty about documentation become a reason to withhold an urgent safety concern.

If your fear is about wording, describe the phenomenon accurately and ask the clinician to explain the working formulation. A record that says "unwanted intrusive harm obsessions, no intent, compulsive avoidance" communicates something different from a single decontextualized phrase. The clinician controls their documentation, but you can provide the context they need.

In a Nutshell

Disclosure is not a magic phrase and it is not a confession ritual. It is the transfer of clinically useful information.

A competent assessment looks beyond the content of a harm thought. It considers whether the thought is unwanted, how you understand it, whether there is intent or a plan, whether psychotic symptoms are present, what compulsions follow, how you are functioning, and what other mental health or safety factors exist.

Safeguarding rules vary. No book can promise what will happen in an individual case. Mental illness or intrusive content alone does not mechanically settle child-protection decisions, and genuine safety concerns still require action.

Your job is not to make the clinician think a particular thing. Your job is to describe the truth clearly enough for a proper assessment.

Chapter 7: What a Clinician Is Listening For

A risk assessment can feel frightening if you imagine the clinician is listening for one wrong word.

A better picture is a set of overlapping questions.

What exactly is happening?

How does the person relate to the thought?

What does she do because of it?

What is her broader mental state?

Is there intent, planning, loss of reality testing, severe mood disturbance, or impaired ability to keep the baby safe?

What support and treatment are needed?

Perinatal OCD consensus recommendations include screening, assessment, differential diagnosis, treatment, and family considerations because the condition sits inside a wider clinical context (Mulcahy et al., 2023). Current perinatal service standards likewise call for assessment of harm-related thoughts while specifically considering that they may be intrusive obsessions (Royal College of Psychiatrists, 2026).

Knowing the domains can make the process less mysterious.

Form: Thought, Image, Urge, Belief, or Voice

The clinician may ask what kind of experience you are having.

A thought may sound like words in your own internal voice.

An image may be a picture in the mind.

An urge may feel like a pull or feared impulse.

A belief is something you take to be true.

A hallucination is a perception-like experience without the usual external source, such as hearing a voice that seems external.

These distinctions are not academic. They help with differential diagnosis.

If you are unsure what category fits, describe the experience instead of choosing a label.

"It was like a picture in my mind, and I knew it was in my mind."

"I heard words that seemed to come from across the room."

"I kept wondering whether I would act, but I did not want to."

"I believed with certainty that the baby had a special supernatural role."

Description gives the assessor more to work with than a label you are guessing at.

Content: What the Mind Says

The clinician may ask for the content.

This is often the hardest part.

Taboo content can include intentional physical harm or sexual harm. You do not have to provide graphic detail to communicate the theme. "I have unwanted sexual-harm images during diaper changes" can be enough to begin.

If the professional needs a clearer description for assessment, answer their questions accurately.

The content matters because it helps identify triggers and risk themes. But content does not stand alone. Hudak and Wisner's clinical discussion of postpartum infant-harm obsessions highlights differential diagnosis rather than treating all harm content as the same phenomenon (Hudak & Wisner, 2012).

Relationship to the Thought

The assessor may ask:

Do you want the thought?

Do you agree with it?

Does it feel alien, unwanted, or inconsistent with you?

Do you believe it predicts what you will do?

Do you fear it might reveal a hidden desire?

Can you consider that your interpretation may be mistaken?

This is where insight and ego-dystonicity become relevant.

Do not aim for the "correct" answer. If your insight fluctuates, say so. "Most of the time I know it is probably OCD, but during a spike I become much less sure."

That is useful clinical information.

Intent and Plan

Expect direct questions about intent.

"Do you intend to harm the baby?"

"Have you made a plan?"

"Have you taken steps toward acting?"

"Do you feel able to keep the baby safe?"

Direct questions can sound accusatory when you are ashamed. They are central to risk assessment.

Answer them as questions, not as moral judgments.

If the answer is no, say no.

If the answer is yes, say yes.

If the answer is "I am terrified that maybe I secretly intend it, but I do not have a wish or plan to act," say that.

If the answer is "I cannot trust myself to remain safe right now," that calls for urgent care.

Compulsions and Avoidance

An OCD assessment should not stop after the obsession.

What happens next may be the clearest part of the pattern.

Do you check?

Wash?

Ask for reassurance?

Avoid infant-care tasks?

Review memories?

Inspect bodily sensations?

Confess?

Research?

Repeat phrases?

Seek a particular feeling?

Estimate the time.

"I spend about two hours a day reviewing."

"I wake my partner to check the baby even after I have already checked."

"I no longer do bath time because of the images."

"I ask for reassurance after almost every diaper change."

Specific behavior is easier to assess than "I am anxious all the time."

Frequency and Duration

A clinician may ask how often the thoughts occur and how long the rituals take.

You do not need perfect data.

A rough, honest pattern is enough.

"Several times during most feeds."

"About ten checking episodes a night."

"Rumination takes one to three hours across the day."

"It started at 30 weeks pregnant and became much worse two weeks after birth."

If OCD makes you count every occurrence, tell the clinician that counting itself has become part of the problem. You do not need to build a forensic log.

Functional Impact

Assessment includes what symptoms are doing to your life.

Can you eat?

Sleep when the baby sleeps and you have the opportunity?

Leave the house?

Complete ordinary infant care?

Work?

Accept help?

Be alone safely?

Concentrate on a conversation?

Do you avoid certain rooms or tasks?

Have relationships become organized around reassurance?

A symptom can deserve treatment even when you are still getting through the day. High-functioning does not mean low distress.

At the same time, major functional collapse can change the urgency and level of care.

Mood

OCD often coexists with depression and other anxiety conditions during the perinatal period (Hudepohl et al., 2022).

The clinician may ask about low mood, loss of pleasure, hopelessness, guilt, agitation, panic, trauma symptoms, irritability, and suicidal thinking.

Do not force every symptom into the OCD explanation.

If you cannot enjoy anything, feel hopeless, or have thoughts of death, tell them. Those symptoms may need attention in their own right.

Psychosis and Mania

Because postpartum psychosis is a medical emergency, assessors may ask about hallucinations, unusual beliefs, confusion, markedly elevated or irritable mood, reduced need for sleep, rapid thoughts or speech, impulsive behavior, and major changes from baseline.

These questions do not mean the clinician has decided you are psychotic.

They mean the differential matters.

NICE advises immediate specialist assessment when symptoms suggest postpartum psychosis (NICE, 2014/2020). The clinician therefore has a reason to ask directly rather than assume.

Sleep

"How are you sleeping?" is not a throwaway question.

The answer needs context.

"I am up every two hours because the baby feeds, and I am exhausted."

"I have a chance to sleep for six hours because my partner has the baby, but I cannot stop reviewing my thoughts."

"I have barely slept for three nights and I do not feel tired. I feel unusually powerful and my family says I am talking much faster."

Those are different patterns.

Sleep loss can worsen coping and distress. A markedly reduced need for sleep in a broader manic or psychotic picture raises different concerns. Describe the opportunity to sleep as well as the hours you got.

Medical and Substance Factors

Pregnancy and postpartum involve physical changes, medications, pain, complications, and sometimes substance use. A mental health assessment may include medical history, current medication, recent medication changes, alcohol or drug use, and obstetric events.

This is not because a clinician thinks your symptoms are imaginary.

It is because assessment should consider causes and contributors outside one diagnostic category.

Bring an accurate medication list.

If you recently started, stopped, or changed a medication, include the date.

History

You may be asked about earlier OCD symptoms, anxiety, depression, bipolar disorder, psychosis, trauma, eating disorders, previous perinatal episodes, psychiatric admissions, and family mental health history.

Fairbrother and colleagues found substantial perinatal OCD prevalence in a prospective cohort, and reviews describe both new onset and exacerbation of existing OCD during pregnancy and postpartum (Fairbrother et al., 2021; Hudepohl et al., 2022).

A history of subtle compulsions before pregnancy may help the clinician understand the current pattern.

It does not mean you caused the episode.

Infant Care and the Relationship

The clinician may ask how feeding, diapering, sleep, bathing, holding, and soothing are going.

They may ask whether you are avoiding the baby, overchecking, or struggling to complete care.

They may ask about attachment or feelings toward the baby.

Answer behaviorally where possible.

"I can do feeds but I avoid diaper changes."

"I hold the baby, but I spend the whole time checking whether I feel love."

"My partner has taken over baths because I am afraid of the thoughts."

These answers show how symptoms interact with caregiving.

Support

Who lives with you?

Who can help?

Is your partner available?

Are there safe relatives or friends nearby?

Is there domestic violence or coercion?

Do you have financial or housing stress?

Can someone help you sleep?

Support is part of safety and treatment planning.

If home is not safe, say so. A plan that assumes a supportive partner is useless when the partner is controlling or violent.

Your Own Questions Belong in the Assessment

An assessment is not an interrogation you pass or fail.

Ask:

"What diagnosis or diagnoses are you considering?"

"What makes you think this is or is not OCD?"

"How are you thinking about psychosis and risk?"

"What treatment do you recommend?"

"Do you offer ERP or refer to someone who does?"

"What should make me seek urgent help between appointments?"

"What are the confidentiality and safeguarding rules here?"

A clear clinician should be able to explain the reasoning at a level you can understand, within the limits of what is known after the assessment.

Make a One-Page Timeline

Before the visit, create one page.

Before pregnancy: relevant mental health history, if any.

During pregnancy: when the first intrusive thoughts or compulsions appeared or changed.

Birth and early postpartum: major medical events and when symptoms shifted.

Now: main obsessions, main compulsions, time spent, tasks affected, mood, sleep, intent or no intent, psychotic symptoms or none, medication, supports.

Keep it brief.

The purpose is to reduce memory load.

Do not spend hours making the timeline perfect. If you cannot remember a date, write "approximately."

What a Good Assessment Gives You

A good assessment does not necessarily give you certainty about every future risk.

It gives you a working clinical formulation.

It identifies what needs urgent action and what can be treated in outpatient care.

It distinguishes obsessional fear from other symptoms as far as the available information allows.

It produces a treatment and safety plan.

It tells you who to contact if symptoms change.

That is enough to move from private investigation to shared clinical care.

The Difference Between Screening and Diagnosis

You may be given a questionnaire.

A screening tool can identify symptoms that deserve closer assessment. It does not, by itself, establish the full diagnosis or risk formulation.

This matters because a frightened parent may treat a score as a verdict.

A low score can be misleading if shame caused you to omit the taboo content.

A high score can indicate significant symptoms without telling the clinician which condition explains them.

Use questionnaires as one source of information. Answer honestly. Then provide the narrative that a score cannot capture: what the thought feels like, what you do afterward, whether there is intent, whether reality testing has changed, and how symptoms affect care.

Why the Clinician May Ask the Same Question Twice

Repetition in an assessment does not necessarily mean disbelief.

The clinician may be clarifying wording, checking consistency, separating an obsession from an intention, or returning to safety after gathering more context.

If the repetition increases fear, ask:

"Can you tell me what distinction you are trying to understand?"

That question can turn a mysterious assessment into a collaborative one.

Do not change an accurate answer simply because you think the first version sounded bad.

What to Do If You Leave Without a Clear Plan

Before the appointment ends, ask for the next step in plain language.

Who is responsible for the referral?

When should you expect contact?

What should you do while waiting?

What symptoms mean you should seek urgent help rather than wait?

Who handles medication questions?

If the plan is unclear after you leave, one practical clarification message is reasonable. Endless interpretation of what the clinician "must have meant" is not.

Write the plan. Then let the appointment be finished.

The Assessment May Change Over Time

A working formulation is not a permanent label stamped on one appointment.

Symptoms can change.

A parent initially presenting with obsessional thoughts may later develop depression that needs separate treatment. A medication change may alter sleep or agitation. A new psychotic symptom would change urgency. An exposure plan may reveal a compulsion that was not visible at first.

Follow-up matters because risk and treatment are based on the current picture.

This is another reason not to demand that the first assessment predict the entire year. Ask instead, "What are we watching, and when will we review it?"

That question turns uncertainty into a monitoring plan without asking for a guarantee.

One Useful Sentence About Uncertainty

If you cannot answer a clinical question with confidence, uncertainty itself is useful data.

"I am not sure whether I believe the thought or only fear it."

"I am not sure whether I slept because I lost track of time."

"I am not sure whether that experience felt internal or external."

Do not force a yes or no to sound decisive. A clinician can ask follow-up questions. Accuracy includes saying when you do not know.

Principles to Remember

A clinician listens for a pattern, not a single shocking sentence.

Useful domains include the form and content of the thought, your relationship to it, intent and planning, compulsions, avoidance, insight, mood, psychotic symptoms, sleep, function, history, medical factors, infant care, and support.

Direct questions about harm or suicide are part of assessment. Answer accurately rather than trying to shape a particular diagnosis.

You can bring a one-page timeline and your own questions. You do not need perfect recall.

The aim of assessment is a plan based on the whole presentation, not a moral verdict about the fact that your mind produced unwanted content.

Chapter 8: Getting the Right Help

The first therapist Grace called said, "We can work on replacing those negative thoughts with positive ones."

Grace wanted that to work. For a week she answered every harm image with a picture of herself as a gentle mother. The positive image gave a quick drop in anxiety, then became another thing she had to do correctly.

When the original thought returned, she felt as if treatment had failed.

The problem was not that positive thoughts are bad. The problem was that the intervention was being used as a neutralizing ritual in a disorder maintained by attempts to get rid of doubt.

OCD treatment needs to address the obsession-compulsion cycle, not merely make the thought sound nicer.

Exposure and response prevention, or ERP, is a form of cognitive behavioral therapy and is widely regarded as a first-line psychological treatment for OCD. The International OCD Foundation describes ERP as approaching feared thoughts, images, situations, or objects while reducing compulsive responses (International OCD Foundation, n.d.). Perinatal OCD reviews and consensus recommendations support using established OCD treatments while adapting care to pregnancy, postpartum needs, comorbidity, and family context (Hudepohl et al., 2022; Mulcahy et al., 2023).

Your task is not to become an expert before making a first call. You need enough knowledge to recognize whether a clinician understands the problem you are bringing.

General Therapy Is Not the Same as OCD Treatment

A thoughtful general therapist can provide support, recognize depression, help with a difficult birth, and be an important part of care. But OCD has treatment-specific features.

Some common therapeutic habits can accidentally feed compulsions when used without attention to function.

Repeatedly debating whether the thought is true can become rumination.

Repeatedly telling you that you are a good person can become reassurance.

Trying to suppress unwanted thoughts can increase monitoring.

Avoiding every trigger can strengthen the belief that the trigger requires special protection.

A clinician who treats OCD should understand this risk.

That does not mean every sentence in therapy must feel uncertain or uncomfortable. Psychoeducation, warmth, problem solving, grief work, trauma treatment, and practical support can all have a place. The key is that the OCD portion of treatment does not build a larger reassurance system.

What ERP Actually Asks You to Learn

People sometimes describe ERP as "face your fear until it goes away."

That description is incomplete.

An exposure brings you into contact with a feared cue, thought, image, situation, or uncertainty. Response prevention asks you to reduce the ritual or avoidance you usually use afterward. Over repeated practice, you learn that you can function without the compulsion and that anxiety or uncertainty does not have to dictate behavior.

The goal is not to prove that nothing bad can ever happen.

It is not to make a therapist certify that you are safe before every exposure.

It is not to stay in a situation until you feel exactly zero anxiety.

Contemporary ERP practice may focus on learning new associations and increasing tolerance of uncertainty rather than treating immediate anxiety reduction as the only marker of success.

The practical message for this book is simple: success is doing the planned, proportionate behavior without the compulsive add-on.

The Perinatal Adaptation

Pregnancy and infant care change logistics.

A parent may be recovering from surgery.

Feeding schedules may be demanding.

A baby may have genuine medical needs.

Sleep may be fragmented.

A therapist cannot design exposure as if those facts are irrelevant.

Perinatal OCD consensus recommendations address case-care factors and treatment decisions specific to the perinatal period, including family context and differential diagnosis (Mulcahy et al., 2023).

Good adaptation does not mean avoiding all anxiety because the person is postpartum. It means separating real medical or infant-care requirements from OCD rituals and choosing practice that fits the person's current capacity.

An exposure should not ask you to violate pediatric guidance.

It should not ask you to ignore a medical restriction.

It should not turn severe sleep deprivation into a test of will.

It should target the unnecessary layer OCD has added.

Three Questions for a Therapist

Before you commit, ask three questions.

"How do you treat OCD when the main theme is unwanted harm thoughts?"

Listen for ERP or another evidence-based OCD approach. A clinician should be able to discuss mental compulsions, reassurance, and avoidance, not only relaxation.

"How do you distinguish intrusive harm obsessions from actual intent or postpartum psychosis?"

A thoughtful answer should mention assessment, insight or reality testing, intent, planning, psychotic symptoms, mood, function, and safety. Be cautious with anyone who says either "all harm thoughts are harmless" or "any harm thought means you cannot be with your baby."

"How would you adapt ERP for pregnancy or early postpartum life?"

Listen for attention to genuine safety, feeding and sleep demands, medical status, support, and collaboration with perinatal clinicians when needed.

You are not looking for a rehearsed slogan. You are listening for clinical reasoning.

Questions About Taboo Themes

If your obsession involves intentional violence or sexual harm, ask directly whether the clinician has treated taboo OCD themes.

Some therapists have excellent general OCD training but little perinatal experience. Others know perinatal anxiety well but have limited ERP experience. If possible, find someone with both.

If that combination is not available, care can still be coordinated. An OCD specialist and a perinatal prescriber or maternity clinician can each contribute within their roles.

The important thing is that nobody treats the taboo content as too embarrassing to discuss.

What a Treatment Plan May Include

A treatment plan is individual, but common elements can include:

Psychoeducation about OCD and intrusive thoughts.

Identification of obsessions, compulsions, avoidance, and reassurance.

A graded exposure plan.

Response prevention for visible and mental rituals.

Work on uncertainty and thought-action fusion.

Reduction of family accommodation.

Monitoring for depression, psychosis, suicide risk, and other comorbid conditions.

Medication discussion when appropriate.

Relapse planning.

The exact sequence depends on severity and context. Do not use a generic list to decide what you "should" be doing without assessment.

When Treatment Feels Like Reassurance Withdrawal

Jordan had relied on their partner for certainty twenty times a day. The therapist suggested reducing those questions.

Jordan felt abandoned.

This is a predictable difficulty. When reassurance has been functioning as a compulsion, reducing it can feel like losing support precisely when distress is high.

A good treatment plan replaces certainty-giving with other forms of support.

The partner can sit nearby.

They can help with practical baby care.

They can remind Jordan of the treatment plan once.

They can ask whether there is new safety information or the old OCD question.

The relationship remains available. The ritual changes.

What If ERP Sounds Dangerous?

For a parent with harm OCD, the word *exposure* can sound like "put the baby at risk to prove a point."

That is not responsible ERP.

Exposure targets fear while preserving ordinary safety.

If the obsession is "What if I have a violent thought while holding my baby?", an exposure may involve ordinary holding that you have been avoiding, with a clinician's guidance and no extra checking. It does not involve creating a dangerous situation.

If the obsession concerns diapering, exposure may involve completing ordinary care without emotional testing or unnecessary transfer to another adult.

If the obsession concerns the kitchen, the plan might start with being in the room while the baby is safely situated, then progress toward ordinary tasks based on the individual's formulation.

The details should be planned with a qualified clinician when the theme is severe or safety feels confusing.

ERP should reduce unnecessary rules, not remove real ones.

When You Need More Than Weekly Outpatient Therapy

Some people need a higher level of care.

That can happen when symptoms consume much of the day, the person cannot complete basic care, depression or suicide risk is significant, psychosis is suspected, medical complications are present, or outpatient treatment is not enough.

Levels of care vary by country and region. They may include more frequent outpatient sessions, intensive outpatient programs, day programs, specialist perinatal services, crisis teams, or inpatient care. In some health systems, specialist mother-and-baby psychiatric units allow treatment while preserving parent-infant contact when clinically appropriate.

Needing more support is a treatment decision, not a score of how hard you tried.

If your clinician recommends a higher level of care, ask what problem it is meant to address, how safety will be managed, what contact with your baby is possible, and how the step-down plan works.

When a Clinician Misunderstands

Suppose you disclose an unwanted violent obsession and the clinician looks alarmed.

Do not assume the story is over.

Ask what they are hearing.

"I want to make sure I described this accurately. The image is unwanted. I am afraid of what it means. I do not have a plan or intention to act. I avoid holding the baby and ask for reassurance afterward. How are you understanding that pattern?"

If you do have intent, do not use that script. State the actual concern.

If the clinician remains unfamiliar with OCD, ask whether they can consult or refer.

You can also bring a reputable perinatal OCD resource, but do not use it to overrule a legitimate risk assessment. The goal is shared clarity.

What Good Treatment Does Not Promise

Good treatment does not promise that you will never have another intrusive thought.

It does not promise perfect certainty about risk.

It does not promise a particular timeline.

It does not make normal parenting stress disappear.

Recovery is measured more usefully by function.

You spend less time ritualizing.

You avoid less.

You can disclose accurately.

The thought has less authority over your choices.

You can return to ordinary care without first resolving every internal question.

A First-Call Script

If calling feels difficult, use this:

"I am pregnant/postpartum and having unwanted intrusive thoughts about harm to my baby. I am worried about OCD. I do not want to use the phone call for reassurance, but I need an assessment. Does your clinician treat OCD with ERP and have experience with perinatal or taboo harm themes?"

If the receptionist cannot answer, ask whether the clinician can reply briefly before booking.

For a prescriber:

"I am having significant obsessive-compulsive symptoms during pregnancy/postpartum. I would like an assessment of treatment options that considers both OCD and perinatal medication factors."

Keep the purpose practical.

Choosing Between Two Imperfect Options

You may not find the ideal clinician immediately.

One therapist may know ERP but not perinatal care.

Another may know perinatal mental health but not OCD treatment.

A third may have a wait list.

Choose the option that gets competent assessment started while you continue looking for the right treatment fit. Ask whether providers can coordinate.

Do not wait for a perfect system before telling someone you are struggling.

If you have urgent symptoms, use urgent services rather than waiting for a specialist appointment.

The Role of Peer Support

Peer groups can reduce secrecy and help people find resources.

They can also become reassurance markets if everyone answers each new obsession with certainty.

Use peer support for connection, practical service information, and shared experience.

Be cautious about posting the same "Does this mean I am dangerous?" question repeatedly. A stranger online cannot perform a risk assessment, and repeated answers may feed the cycle.

A healthy peer space should be able to say, "That sounds distressing. Please discuss risk with your clinician, and if this is OCD, the certainty question may be part of the problem."

Action: Interview the Treatment, Not Yourself

Write the three therapist questions from this chapter.

Add one question specific to your circumstances.

Perhaps:

"How do you work with mental compulsions?"

"Can partners join a session to learn how to reduce reassurance?"

"How do you coordinate with an OB-GYN or psychiatrist?"

Then make one contact.

Afterward, do not grade the call for whether you sounded like the "right kind" of patient.

Grade it on one behavior: did you provide enough information to move toward appropriate care?

Signs That Therapy Is Targeting the Right Problem

You do not have to judge treatment by whether every session makes you feel better immediately.

Look for process.

Does the clinician identify the obsession-compulsion loop?

Can they name mental rituals as well as visible ones?

Do they help you approach ordinary situations that OCD has taken away?

Do they reduce reassurance rather than supplying more sophisticated reassurance?

Do they distinguish genuine safety from OCD rules?

Do they ask about depression, psychosis, suicidality, sleep, and other conditions when relevant?

Do you leave with a behavioral practice rather than only a new explanation to analyze?

Treatment can still be difficult when these elements are present. The signs tell you that the work is pointed at the maintaining mechanism.

When Progress Is Hard to See

OCD can make treatment progress invisible because it moves the standard.

Last month you would not be alone with the baby. This week you are alone for thirty minutes, but the mind says thirty minutes proves nothing.

Last month you asked for reassurance fifteen times a day. Now you ask five times, but the mind says five is still too many.

Use concrete behavior.

What can you do now that you could not do before?

Which ritual is shorter?

Which topic can you disclose more accurately?

How quickly do you return after a spike?

Progress does not need to be complete to be real.

If there is no behavioral change after a reasonable treatment period, discuss that openly. The plan may need adjustment.

If Treatment Access Is Delayed

Wait lists create a difficult gap.

Use the wait to prepare rather than to run endless self-tests.

Keep the appointment guide.

Ask whether the service has cancellation slots.

Ask your primary or maternity clinician what support is available while you wait.

Use reputable OCD education.

Reduce one low-risk reassurance habit if you can do so without confusing it with a genuine safety issue.

Do not design severe exposures from internet examples.

If symptoms worsen, tell the referring clinician. A wait-list position does not prevent reassessment of urgency.

If urgent signs appear, use urgent services rather than waiting for the scheduled specialist.

Principles to Remember

ERP is a first-line psychological treatment for OCD. In perinatal care, the principles are adapted to real medical, infant-care, family, and sleep conditions rather than applied mechanically.

A therapist who treats harm OCD should understand mental compulsions, reassurance, avoidance, uncertainty, and differential diagnosis.

Exposure does not mean creating danger. Ordinary safety stays in place while OCD-only rules are reduced.

Support remains important even when reassurance rituals are changed.

The right treatment does not make you prove who you are. It helps you change what you do when uncertainty arrives.

Chapter 9: The SAFE Return

A method for a frightened new parent has to survive real life.

It has to work when the baby is crying.

It has to work when you have one hand free.

It has to work after a thought so shame-filled that every instinct says, *Stop everything and solve this.*

That is what the SAFE Return is for.

It does not tell you whether you have OCD. It does not replace risk assessment. It does not replace therapist-guided ERP. It gives you a direction in the small interval between an intrusive thought and the compulsion that usually follows.

S: Spot the obsession.

A: Allow uncertainty.

F: Forego the compulsion.

E: Engage with real care.

The word *return* matters. You are not trying to win an internal debate. You are returning to the life and task that OCD interrupted.

S: Spot the Obsession

Maya was washing a bottle when an image appeared.

The old response was to ask, "Why that image?"

The SAFE Return begins earlier.

"That is the threat question again."

Spotting means recognizing form and pattern without conducting a diagnosis each time.

You might say:

"Intrusive image."

"Possibility question."

"Responsibility alarm."

"Same OCD theme."

Use ordinary language. Say it once.

Do not repeat the label until you feel calm. The label is a signpost, not a neutralizing phrase.

Spotting also means noticing when the obsession is disguised as a practical question.

"What if I did not clean this correctly?"

Sometimes that is a real practical question. If you followed the normal cleaning steps and no new information has appeared, the repeated question may be obsessional.

The context tells you more than the wording.

When You Cannot Tell Whether It Is OCD

There will be moments when you are unsure.

Do not use the SAFE Return to dismiss a legitimate safety concern.

If there is new evidence of an actual problem, address it.

The baby has a fever: follow medical guidance.

The car-seat buckle is visibly undone: fasten it.

You are so drowsy you cannot safely hold the baby: put the baby in a safe place or hand care to another adult.

You are hearing a voice telling you to harm the baby: seek urgent medical assessment.

The SAFE Return is for the extra obsessional demand that remains after proportionate action is clear.

If you repeatedly cannot tell the difference, bring specific examples to an OCD-trained clinician and build agreed stopping rules.

A: Allow Uncertainty

This step is usually the least popular.

OCD says, "Before you continue, know."

Know what the thought means.

Know what you will feel tomorrow.

Know what you would do in every imaginable circumstance.

Know that nobody could misunderstand you.

Know that no accident could occur.

Allowing uncertainty means declining that demand.

It does not mean saying that harm is acceptable.

It means admitting that human beings do not get perfect knowledge about every future event or internal state.

A response can be:

"I do not get complete certainty here."

"Maybe the feeling will stay strange for a while."

"I can leave that question unanswered."

"I am not solving the identity question."

Notice that these phrases do not contain reassurance.

They are permission to stop the search.

Uncertainty Is Not the Same as Risk

This distinction is worth repeating.

Uncertainty is a property of knowledge. Risk is a judgment about the probability and seriousness of a possible event using available information.

You can have uncertainty with low risk.

You can have uncertainty with high risk.

You can have a situation that requires immediate action despite uncertainty.

The OCD trap is treating any remaining uncertainty as proof that risk has not been managed.

Ordinary safety accepts a stopping point.

OCD says the stopping point is irresponsible because certainty is not complete.

Allowing uncertainty means obeying the proportionate stopping point anyway.

F: Forego the Compulsion

This is the behavioral center.

After spotting the obsession and allowing uncertainty, identify what you usually do next.

Check.

Ask.

Review.

Avoid.

Confess.

Search.

Test.

Replace the thought.

Monitor your feelings.

Then do less of that.

"Forego" can mean drop the ritual entirely when you are ready. It can also mean shorten or delay it as part of a graded plan.

If you normally ask your partner five times, ask once less.

If you review for thirty minutes, stop after noticing the first loop.

If you avoid diapering, work with your therapist on a graded return.

If you search forums for an hour, set the phone down when you notice the purpose is reassurance.

Response prevention is not a mood. You can feel very anxious and still have completed it.

What If the Compulsion Is in Your Head?

Mental compulsions require a different kind of stopping.

You cannot force your mind to become silent.

You can stop voluntarily extending the analysis.

Suppose the thought is, "What if that image meant I wanted it?"

The first mental response may arrive automatically.

"No, I hated it."

Then you notice the loop beginning.

Rather than supplying five more arguments, say, "I am not continuing the review."

Your mind may answer on its own. Let it.

You are not responsible for preventing every internal sentence.

You are practicing not *participating* in the ritual.

E: Engage With Real Care

This step prevents the method from becoming an exercise in sitting still and waiting for anxiety to disappear.

Return to a real action.

Fasten the sleeper.

Finish the feed.

Push the stroller.

Make the appointment.

Hand your partner the grocery list.

Take the nap someone has made possible.

Complete the ordinary diaper change.

Real care can be directed at the baby, yourself, your household, your relationship, or treatment.

The action does not have to feel tender.

It has to be proportionate and chosen.

"But I Still Feel Terrible"

You may.

The SAFE Return does not promise immediate relief.

If you judge it by whether anxiety falls in two minutes, you may turn it into another ritual.

Judge it by behavior.

Did you label once rather than investigate?

Did you allow the unanswered question?

Did you reduce the compulsion?

Did you return to the next real task?

That is a completed repetition even if your body still feels alarmed.

The Method During Diapering

Nia's trigger was diapering.

An unwanted sexual image appeared. She froze.

Old sequence: check bodily sensation, feel disgust, ask her partner to finish, then search online.

SAFE Return:

Spot: "Intrusive image."

Allow: "I am not deciding what this says about me."

Forego: no body check, no partner reassurance, no search.

Engage: complete the ordinary diaper change according to normal care.

If Nia has never done this and distress is extreme, her therapist may grade the exposure. Perhaps she begins with the partner nearby but not reassuring. Later the partner leaves the room. The exact hierarchy is individual.

The principle stays the same.

The Method With Accidental Harm

Elena fears stairs.

Every time she carries the baby near them, an image of falling appears.

Old sequence: put the baby down, call her partner, avoid that part of the house.

With a therapist, Elena confirms ordinary stair safety: appropriate footwear, handrail use, not carrying the baby when medically dizzy or dangerously fatigued.

Then SAFE Return:

Spot: "The fall image."

Allow: "I cannot obtain a guarantee about every step."

Forego: no mental replay of whether her grip is perfect.

Engage: use the stairs in the ordinary safe way if that is part of the agreed exposure.

The method never tells a dizzy parent to take the stairs. Genuine conditions change the real rule.

The Method With Contamination

Samira cleans a bottle according to the current instructions she was given by her pediatric or public-health source.

Then doubt arrives: "Maybe there was residue."

She wants to start again.

Spot: "Repeat-cleaning doubt."

Allow: "The ordinary procedure is done. I may still feel uncertain."

Forego: no second wash solely for the feeling.

Engage: move to the next care task.

If there is actual new contamination, she handles it. OCD is not an excuse to ignore evidence.

The skill is stopping when the real task is complete.

The Method With Disclosure

The SAFE Return can be used before an appointment.

Spot: "If I say the actual thought, the clinician will certainly think the worst."

Allow: "I cannot control the clinician's first reaction or guarantee the outcome."

Forego: do not rewrite the disclosure until it sounds harmless.

Engage: bring the accurate six-sentence script and ask for assessment.

This may be among the harder exposures in the book.

It is also highly practical.

The Method With Reassurance

Rachel texts her sister after every intrusive thought.

She types, "Please tell me I would never do anything."

Before sending:

Spot: "Reassurance request."

Allow: "I want certainty and I am not going to get permanent certainty from this text."

Forego: delete the question.

Engage: if she needs connection, send a different message: "Rough OCD moment. Can we talk about something ordinary for ten minutes?"

Connection remains.

Certainty-giving changes.

Do Not Ritualize SAFE

Any useful OCD tool can become part of OCD.

You might feel you must say all four steps perfectly.

You might repeat them until anxiety drops.

You might ask your therapist whether you "did SAFE right."

You might write S-A-F-E on paper twenty times after a thought.

That is the system being pulled into the old function.

Use the lightest version that works.

Sometimes the entire method is:

"Threat question. No review. Back to feeding."

That counts.

The goal is less ceremony around the thought.

What SAFE Cannot Do

It cannot diagnose psychosis.

It cannot determine whether a baby has a medical problem.

It cannot decide whether you are safe to drive when sleep deprived.

It cannot replace a prescriber.

It cannot resolve a safeguarding decision.

It cannot make intent disappear if intent is present.

For those situations, real care means contacting the relevant professional or emergency service.

The E in SAFE is partly a protection against misusing the method. "Engage with real care" means respond to actual needs with actual care.

A One-Card Version

Write this once on a small card or phone note:

Spot: Name the obsession once.

Allow: Leave the certainty question open.

Forego: Drop or reduce the ritual.

Engage: Do the next ordinary, safe, chosen action.

Underneath, add:

Emergency exception: New intent, plan, psychotic symptoms, severe confusion or mania, or inability to maintain safety means urgent professional assessment.

Do not keep editing the card.

It is meant to simplify.

Measuring Progress

At the end of a week, do not count how many intrusive thoughts you had.

Count choices.

How many times did you shorten a reassurance exchange?

How many avoided tasks did you re-enter with your therapist's plan?

How often did you stop the second round of rumination?

How often did you follow the ordinary safety rule once?

This measure can show progress even during a week when thoughts feel loud.

Recovery is not thought eradication.

It is increasing freedom from compulsory response.

SAFE When the Thought Is Not Clearly an Obsession

The method works best after you and your clinician have identified a recurring OCD pattern.

If a thought is genuinely new and you cannot tell whether it reflects an obsession, a medical concern, a mood change, psychosis, or intent, the E step changes the direction.

Engage with real care may mean contacting the clinician.

It may mean telling your partner, "This is different from my usual pattern."

It may mean seeking urgent assessment.

SAFE is not a machine for labeling every frightening event as OCD.

The method is protective only when ordinary and urgent care remain available.

SAFE Without Acronyms

Some people dislike acronyms.

You can use the same method in one sentence:

"Notice the threat question, leave certainty open, skip the ritual, return to the real task."

Or even:

"Notice. Do less OCD. Do the next real thing."

The wording does not matter.

The behavioral direction does.

If memorizing four letters becomes another test, use plain language.

When the Return Feels Flat

Sometimes you return to the baby and feel no relief.

Sometimes the task feels mechanical.

That can be discouraging if you expected response prevention to produce a reward.

The reward is not a guaranteed feeling. The practice is the fact that OCD did not choose the behavior.

A feed completed while anxious is still a feed.

An appointment booked while uncertain is still booked.

A reassurance question not asked is still a changed response.

Let those facts be enough for the repetition.

SAFE With a Partner Nearby

A partner can support the method without becoming part of it.

The parent says, "I am getting the reassurance urge."

The partner replies, "I hear you. What is the next real task?"

The parent chooses the action.

The partner does not supply the answer to the obsession.

This matters because the SAFE Return should increase the parent's ability to choose behavior, not create a new ritual in which the partner recites four steps.

If you need prompting at first, use one prompt. Gradually remove it.

SAFE After You Already Performed the Compulsion

Sometimes you notice the cycle late.

You searched.

You asked.

You reviewed.

Do not start a second ritual about having ritualized.

Spot: "I just did the compulsion."

Allow: "I do not need to know how much damage that did to recovery."

Forego: do not repeat it or analyze the mistake.

Engage: return to the next real task.

The method still works after an imperfect moment.

When the Method Feels Too Simple

OCD problems can be elaborate, so a four-step response may seem insufficient.

The simplicity is intentional.

The SAFE Return does not contain the whole formulation, hierarchy, risk assessment, or medication plan. Those live elsewhere in care.

It only answers the moment-level question: what direction should behavior move after a familiar obsession appears?

If the situation requires more than that, use more care.

If it does not, resist adding ten extra steps merely because anxiety feels serious.

A small response repeated in ordinary life can carry more learning than a complicated ritualized protocol.

In a Nutshell

The SAFE Return is a four-step memory aid: Spot the obsession, Allow uncertainty, Forego the compulsion, Engage with real care.

Spot once. Do not turn labeling into analysis.

Allowing uncertainty does not mean ignoring risk. Follow real safety rules and respond to new evidence. Leave the extra certainty demand unanswered.

Foregoing a compulsion can be complete or graded. Mental rituals count.

Engaging means returning to a real task rather than waiting for the right feeling.

Use the method lightly. If it becomes elaborate, repetitive, or aimed at producing certainty, simplify it.

Chapter 10: ERP in Two-Minute Windows

The phrase "therapy homework" can sound absurd when you are measuring the day in feeds.

An exposure plan that requires forty-five quiet minutes may be reasonable for one person and unusable for another.

That does not mean early parenthood makes ERP impossible.

Many compulsions happen during ordinary care. That means response prevention can also happen there.

A two-minute window is not a promise that OCD can be treated in two minutes. It is a unit of practice. The full treatment may involve regular sessions, longer exposures, medication, family work, and sustained repetition over weeks or months. The window simply answers a practical question: *What can I practice when life is fragmented?*

ERP in One Sentence

Approach the feared cue or uncertainty in a planned, proportionate way and reduce the ritual you usually use to feel safe.

That is the basic direction.

The International OCD Foundation describes ERP as exposure to thoughts, images, objects, or situations that provoke obsessions, paired with choosing not to perform the compulsive response (International OCD Foundation, n.d.).

The details matter.

Good ERP is not reckless exposure.

It is not white-knuckling.

It is not a test of character.

It is not "do the most frightening thing first."

It is planned learning.

Build the Target From a Compulsion

Start with behavior, not the most shocking image.

Pick one compulsion that interferes with ordinary care.

Repeatedly checking the baby after safe-sleep placement.

Asking your partner whether you seemed dangerous during a feed.

Avoiding the room where the intrusive thought first occurred.

Rewashing an already-clean item.

Checking bodily sensations during diapering.

The exposure is often hiding inside the life you stopped living.

If you avoid holding the baby in a certain chair, sitting in the chair may become an exposure.

If you wash twice, washing once according to the real rule and stopping may be the exposure.

If you ask five reassurance questions, asking fewer may be response prevention.

Make a Small Ladder

A hierarchy orders practice from easier to harder.

You do not need twenty items.

Start with three.

For example, a parent who avoids being alone with the baby after violent intrusive images might create, with her therapist:

Step one: complete a routine feed while the partner is in the next room, with no reassurance afterward.

Step two: complete a short care routine while the partner takes a walk nearby, with agreed phone boundaries.

Step three: spend a longer ordinary period caring for the baby while the partner is away, following normal safety plans.

The exact steps depend on the person's assessment. If there is actual risk, psychosis, severe impairment, or another safety issue, this hierarchy may be inappropriate.

That is why severe or confusing presentations belong with a clinician.

Do Not Use Distress Scores as Pass or Fail

Many ERP plans use a subjective distress rating.

That can help organize a hierarchy.

OCD can also turn the number into a performance score.

"I was still at a seven after ten minutes, so I failed."

"I only felt a three. Maybe the exposure was fake."

"I need to repeat it until the number reaches zero."

The better question is behavioral:

Did I approach what the plan asked me to approach?

Did I reduce the compulsion?

Did I remain within ordinary safety?

Did I return to life afterward?

Anxiety may rise, fall, wobble, or remain steady during one practice. Learning occurs across repetition, not only when a single session ends peacefully.

A Two-Minute Window During Feeding

Sofia has an intrusive image during bottle feeding.

Her usual compulsion is mental review.

For two minutes she practices:

Notice the image.

Leave the "what does it mean?" question unanswered.

Keep feeding according to ordinary care.

When the mind begins reviewing, return attention to the physical task without arguing.

At the end of two minutes, she does not ask whether anxiety decreased.

She simply continues the feed.

The practice was not two minutes of trying to relax.

It was two minutes of not conducting the investigation.

A Two-Minute Window After a Check

Hannah checks the baby's sleep setup according to the normal routine.

Doubt arrives.

She wants to check again.

Her window is the first two minutes after walking away.

She stays away from the second check.

She does not stare at a monitor unless the monitor is part of ordinary, proportionate use.

She notices the urge.

She lets it remain.

Then she moves into the next ordinary action.

If she returns after two minutes solely because the doubt remains, she has delayed the compulsion, which may still be a useful first step. The plan can gradually extend the delay until the repeated check is dropped.

A Two-Minute Window for Internet Searching

The urge to search can feel practical.

Set a timer before opening the browser, but only if you have an actual information task.

If the task is reassurance, the exposure is often not searching.

For two minutes, keep the phone where it is.

Read the obsessional question without answering it.

Let uncertainty remain.

Do a real task.

After two minutes, reassess the function.

"Do I need information to make a decision, or do I need a feeling?"

If it is the feeling, continue without the search.

Imaginal Exposure

Some OCD fears cannot be reproduced safely or ethically in real life. Therapists may use imaginal exposure, in which a person deliberately contacts feared thoughts or uncertainty through words, scripts, or images while reducing compulsive neutralization.

Harm OCD often involves exactly this problem. Nobody should create a dangerous real-world situation for exposure.

Imaginal work can therefore help address catastrophic meanings under professional guidance.

Do not write graphic scripts from this book as a solo challenge.

A therapist can choose language that targets the obsession without turning the exercise into self-punishment or a new test.

The important mechanism is willingness to contact feared uncertainty while not neutralizing it.

When the Exposure Becomes a Test

Priya held the baby and thought, "I am doing ERP."

Then she checked whether she felt an urge.

Nothing happened.

Relief.

She repeated the exercise to prove the result.

Now the exposure had become testing.

You can spot this by the desired outcome.

ERP desired outcome: "I will practice ordinary holding while leaving uncertainty unanswered."

Testing desired outcome: "I will hold the baby to prove I do not have an urge."

Same action. Different function.

If you catch the shift, do not panic about doing treatment wrong. Name it and remove the test.

Response Prevention for Rumination

You cannot physically block a thought.

You can refuse to continue a voluntary chain.

Try three moves.

First, identify the question.

"What if I secretly wanted the image?"

Second, identify the operation.

"I am reviewing my reaction for proof."

Third, end the operation.

"I am not doing the next round."

Then attend to the next external action.

The thought may keep speaking.

Response prevention is not silence. It is less deliberate engagement.

The Risk of Reassuring Treatment Language

Even accurate therapy language can become ritualized.

"Thoughts are not actions."

"OCD attacks what matters."

"This is ego-dystonic."

If you repeat these statements every time until anxiety falls, they may be serving the same function as reassurance from a partner.

A therapist may still use psychoeducation. The difference is whether information is helping you understand the treatment model or being dispensed repeatedly as a certainty dose.

The SAFE Return keeps the answer light.

"I notice the obsession. I am leaving the meaning unresolved. Back to the task."

Practice While Sleep Deprived

Sleep deprivation reduces patience and concentration.

Make the task smaller rather than abandoning it.

Drop one reassurance question.

Delay one search.

Complete one routine care task you have been avoiding.

Stop one round of mental review.

Do not choose the hardest exposure during a period of extreme exhaustion simply to prove commitment.

If you are so tired that an activity is physically unsafe, choose safety. Put the baby in a safe place, hand care to another adult, rest, and discuss the pattern with your clinician.

ERP targets OCD avoidance. It does not require ignoring human limits.

Coordinate With Ordinary Infant Safety

Write down the actual rule before practice when confusion is likely.

For a task involving sleep, use current safe-sleep guidance from your pediatric or public-health authority.

For feeding, use the instructions appropriate to your baby's age and medical needs.

For car travel, follow the child-restraint instructions and local law.

For medication, follow your prescriber and pharmacist.

Once the real rule is defined, the exposure targets the additional rule OCD created.

This boundary reduces two errors: treating an OCD demand as safety, and treating real safety as if it were OCD.

What About Repeating an Exposure?

Repetition matters.

The reason to repeat is learning and practice, not because the previous repetition felt imperfect.

A simple schedule may be better than an anxiety-driven one.

"Once a day for five days."

"During the morning feed this week."

"Every other diaper change while my partner is home, then progress."

Agree on the plan with your therapist.

If you find yourself adding unscheduled repetitions because you need to check a reaction, stop and bring that pattern to treatment.

A Three-Step Micro-Ladder

Choose one avoided or ritualized task that is part of ordinary life and is safe for you to perform.

Write three versions.

Easier: one small reduction in the ritual.

Middle: ordinary task with less accommodation.

Harder: ordinary task with the OCD-only rule removed.

Example:

Easier: wash the bottle once according to the real procedure, then wait two minutes before deciding whether to repeat.

Middle: wash once and leave the kitchen.

Harder: wash once, use it as intended, and do not seek reassurance about the process.

The goal is not to make "harder" dramatic.

It is to make it more ordinary.

When to Stop Solo Practice and Ask for Help

Self-directed education can be useful for mild symptoms, but there are limits.

Seek professional help if you are unsure about diagnosis or risk, cannot maintain safety, suspect psychosis or mania, have suicidal intent, have severe depression, are unable to care for yourself or the baby, are rapidly worsening, or find that attempts at exposure are escalating distress without a workable plan.

Also ask for help when OCD has become so elaborate that you cannot identify which behaviors are compulsions.

Treatment is not reserved for people who have failed at self-help.

The Difference Between Courage and Compulsion

OCD can turn recovery into another standard.

"I must do the hardest exposure."

"I must never ask for reassurance again."

"I must feel uncertain perfectly."

"If I avoid once, I ruined the week."

That rigidity is familiar.

A treatment plan can be disciplined without becoming punitive.

If you perform a compulsion, identify what happened and make the next planned practice.

If you discover the hierarchy is too steep, adjust it with your therapist.

If your medical situation changes, revise the plan.

The direction matters more than a flawless streak.

Separate Exposure From Endurance

There is no prize for staying in a practice that has become physically unsafe, medically inappropriate, or so poorly designed that it teaches nothing except panic.

A useful exposure has a target.

"I am practicing holding the baby without checking my grip for hidden intent."

A vague endurance challenge sounds different.

"I must hold the baby no matter what, or I am failing."

If pain, dizziness, extreme fatigue, or another real condition appears, respond to it.

If anxiety alone rises, that may be the very experience the practice is designed to allow.

The distinction should be discussed with the treating clinician when uncertainty is high.

Vary the Practice Gently

Once a small exposure becomes workable, vary one feature.

Different time of day.

Different safe room.

Partner nearby versus farther away.

One ordinary care task followed by another.

Variation can help the learning transfer beyond one exact setup.

Do not vary five things at once.

The point is flexibility, not intensity.

What to Record

If your therapist asks for records, keep them short.

Date.

Planned task.

Compulsion reduced.

What you learned behaviorally.

For example:

"Tuesday. Completed diaper change. Did not check body sensations afterward. Anxiety stayed high for a while and I still finished."

That record is more useful than a page of analysis about whether you believed the thought.

If logging becomes another ritual, tell the therapist and simplify it.

Micro-Practice Is Not the Whole Treatment

A two-minute practice is useful because it can be repeated in a busy day.

It cannot cover everything a therapist may need to do.

Assessment, formulation, hierarchy design, work with family accommodation, medication coordination, comorbid depression or trauma, and higher-risk decisions may require longer clinical work.

Do not interpret the convenience of micro-practice as evidence that severe OCD should be managed alone.

The small window is where a treatment principle meets daily life.

The larger treatment still matters.

When an Exposure Has Become Too Easy

An easy exposure is not useless.

It can keep a skill active.

But if you are completing it with no urge to ritualize and no meaningful uncertainty, it may no longer be the best growth target.

With your therapist, change one variable or move to the next step.

Do not make the new step dramatically harder.

Aim for a task that asks you to give up a little more compulsive control while preserving ordinary safety.

The Window After the Exposure

What happens immediately afterward matters.

You may complete a planned task, then seek reassurance that the task was safe.

You may review whether the exposure "worked."

You may compare anxiety scores for half an hour.

That post-exposure behavior can restore the compulsion you just reduced.

Include the next few minutes in the plan.

Finish the task.

Do not debrief with yourself.

Move into an ordinary activity.

Save treatment questions for the scheduled review unless something genuinely changes.

Principles to Remember

ERP pairs planned contact with feared cues or uncertainty with reduction of compulsive responses. It preserves ordinary safety.

Two-minute windows are units of practice, not a claim that treatment is quick. The practice can happen inside feeding, checking, diapering, internet use, or another routine.

Build exposure from a behavior you want back, then create a small ladder. Measure success by the planned action and response prevention, not by immediate anxiety reduction.

Watch for exposures turning into tests.

Real fatigue, medical restrictions, infant needs, and emergency symptoms change what is appropriate. Good treatment works with reality rather than treating every limit as avoidance.

Chapter 11: Everyday Triggers Without Extra Rules

The house did not become more dangerous when the baby came home.

It became more visible.

Edges, stairs, water, kitchen tools, car seats, changing tables, medicines, cleaning products, sleep positions, and feeding equipment all moved to the foreground. For a new parent, some of that attention is appropriate. Babies depend on adults for basic safety.

For a parent with harm OCD, the same environment can become a map of feared possibilities.

The treatment task is not to stop caring about safety. It is to separate **ordinary safety** from an **OCD safety rule**.

Ordinary safety is proportionate. It comes from reliable guidance, obvious conditions, or practical judgment. It has a stopping point.

An OCD safety rule is an added restriction, check, ritual, or avoidance whose main job is to quiet obsessional doubt.

Those rules can feel almost identical from inside the fear.

Define the Real Rule First

Before reducing a ritual, identify the actual safety requirement.

If the question involves safe sleep, use current pediatric or public-health guidance.

If it involves a medication, use the prescriber and pharmacist.

If it involves a car seat, use the manufacturer's instructions and local requirements.

If it involves a baby's medical condition, follow the baby's clinical team.

If you are unsure whether fatigue or a physical recovery issue makes a task unsafe, ask the relevant clinician.

Then stop moving the standard.

OCD likes to renegotiate after the real rule has been met.

"Yes, the buckle is fastened, but maybe pull it one more time."

"Yes, the bottle was prepared correctly, but perhaps wash your hands again."

"Yes, the baby is in the ordinary safe setup, but check breathing one more time."

The point at which the evidence stops changing and the feeling becomes the reason for another action is often where response prevention starts.

The Staircase

Priya had used the stairs in her house for years.

After one intrusive image of falling while carrying the baby, she stopped.

Her husband brought the baby up and down. Priya told herself this was sensible because stairs can cause accidents. That statement was true in general and still did not explain the new rule. Nothing about the stairs had changed. Priya had not become dizzy, injured, or medically restricted. The difference was the image.

With her therapist, she listed ordinary precautions. She used the handrail. She did not carry the baby when impaired by medication, illness, or extreme fatigue. She wore shoes or went barefoot rather than using slippery socks, based on the conditions of her home.

Then she practiced.

The first exposure was not theatrical. She stood at the bottom while holding the baby in a normal, secure position. She allowed the image to appear without reviewing it.

Later she used several steps.

Eventually she used the staircase as she had intended before OCD took over.

Her target was not to prove that a fall could never happen. Her target was to stop treating the mental image as a new piece of physical evidence.

Bath Time

Water deserves real caution around infants. That is why bath-related OCD can be difficult to untangle.

The ordinary rule is clear in principle: follow age-appropriate bathing guidance and provide the required supervision.

OCD then adds private rules.

Do not bathe the baby unless another adult is in the room.

Do not touch a particular object.

Keep both hands on the baby every second even when the actual setup does not require that exact ritual.

Repeat the water check because the first temperature check did not feel right.

Replay the bath afterward for signs that you could have acted.

If another adult is present because you are learning the task, physically recovering, or sharing work, that may be practical.

If their presence is required solely because an unwanted thought appeared, it may be accommodation.

An ERP plan might reduce the OCD layer gradually. The baby still receives normal supervision. The parent stops using a second adult as a guarantee.

The Kitchen

Kitchen triggers often combine accidental and intentional harm fears.

A parent may stop cooking while the baby is nearby, move ordinary tools to inaccessible places not required by standard household safety, or refuse to be in the room while the partner prepares food.

Start by separating childproofing from self-proofing.

Childproofing asks, "What access does a mobile child have, given age and development?"

Self-proofing asks, "What must I remove so I never have to feel the uncertainty caused by my thought?"

Those are different questions.

If a baby is too young to access a drawer, locking every tool away solely because you fear your own unwanted image may be an OCD safety rule. If a toddler can access the drawer, securing dangerous items is ordinary child safety regardless of your thoughts.

Age, environment, and function matter.

Do not remove reasonable childproofing as an exposure.

Target the rule that was added to manage obsessional fear.

Holding the Baby

For some parents, the trigger is simply contact.

Maya noticed an intrusive image while rocking her baby. She began holding the baby only when seated, then only when her partner was present, then as little as possible.

She told herself the baby seemed content with other caregivers.

The real loss was hers too. Ordinary care had become conditional on feeling safe enough.

A graded return may start with a brief, routine hold while another adult is nearby but not monitoring. The parent agrees not to check grip pressure, emotional warmth, or bodily sensations. Later the support person is farther away. The task lengthens.

The point is not forced closeness.

It is to remove the rule that says an unwanted image controls who may hold the child.

Diapering and Sexual-Harm Obsessions

This is the subject many books soften.

An unwanted sexual image, word, or bodily sensation during diapering can create intense shame. A parent may decide she should never change the baby again. She may check whether touch was "appropriate enough," inspect arousal, replay where her eyes went, or confess every detail afterward.

Sexual obsessions are recognized within OCD presentations, including perinatal OCD resources that describe unwanted sexual and violent thoughts about the baby (Royal College of Psychiatrists, n.d.).

The clinical distinction still matters. Unwanted obsessional content is assessed differently from actual sexual interest, intent, abusive behavior, or psychosis. A book cannot perform that assessment.

If a qualified clinician identifies the pattern as OCD, treatment may involve returning to ordinary diapering while reducing emotional and body checking, repeated confession, and avoidance.

The baby-care task remains exactly that: care.

No graphic exposure content is needed.

Driving

Driving raises a different problem because fatigue and impairment are real safety issues.

An intrusive image about a crash can lead to avoidance even when the parent is alert and competent to drive.

But a severely sleep-deprived person may genuinely be unsafe behind the wheel.

Do not use "this is OCD" to override actual impairment.

Ask the practical question first: am I fit to drive under normal safety standards and any medical restrictions that apply to me?

If yes, the obsessional layer may be: driving only with another adult, taking unnecessarily long routes, repeatedly checking mirrors for evidence of having hit something, or replaying the drive afterward.

If no, choose another transport plan and address the sleep or medical problem.

ERP does not reward ignoring reality.

Strollers and Public Spaces

A stroller walk may trigger images involving roads, strangers, falls, or sudden impulses.

The OCD response can be to stop going out, use only one exact route, avoid bridges or stairs, or grip the stroller so rigidly that the walk becomes an endurance task.

Ordinary safety still applies: use the stroller as designed, obey traffic signals, secure the baby appropriately, and account for weather and local conditions.

The exposure target is the extra rule.

Perhaps you use a slightly different safe route.

Perhaps you stop checking the brake three times after it is set.

Perhaps you cross at an ordinary signal without replaying whether your hands were placed correctly.

Small changes restore flexibility.

Being Alone With the Baby

This can be the largest avoidance.

A parent may arrange for constant supervision not because another adult is needed for medical or practical reasons, but because being alone makes the intrusive thought feel more dangerous.

Before changing that arrangement, assessment matters.

If there is psychosis, intent, severe depression, substance impairment, medical instability, or another real safety concern, supervision may be part of a legitimate plan.

If the pattern is assessed as OCD and the supervision is operating as accommodation, the treatment plan may gradually reduce it.

Start small.

Five minutes while the partner is in another room.

A routine care task while the partner runs a short errand.

A planned period alone that is long enough to practice, not long enough to become an ordeal.

The goal is ordinary parenting capacity, not proving independence.

The "What If I Snap?" Trigger

Many harm obsessions are not tied to an object.

They are tied to emotion.

The baby cries.

You feel anger or panic.

The thought appears: "What if I snap?"

First check the practical situation.

Are you so overwhelmed that you fear losing behavioral control?

If yes, put the baby in an appropriate safe place, step away, get another adult, and seek help as needed. If you have actual intent to harm or cannot maintain safety, seek urgent care.

If the thought is an unwanted obsession and you are behaviorally safe, the OCD layer may be repeated checking of anger.

"Am I at 20 percent anger or 30?"

"Did I clench my jaw?"

"Did I enjoy the silence after the baby stopped crying?"

Do not use emotional monitoring as a safety instrument.

Use behavior and a real plan.

Sleep-Related Checking

New parents often check babies.

OCD can turn checking into a schedule that no one prescribed.

Hannah checked the baby's breathing after every small sound and often after no sound at all. The check relieved fear for a moment, then made the next uncertainty harder.

Her therapist helped her identify what monitoring was actually recommended for her healthy baby and what she had added.

Response prevention began with one omitted extra check.

Not all readers will have the same ordinary rule. Premature infants, babies with health conditions, and medical monitoring plans change the situation.

Do not borrow another parent's stopping rule.

Use the rule appropriate to your baby.

Then notice what OCD adds.

"But Good Parents Are Extra Careful"

OCD likes the word *extra*.

Extra checking looks loving.

Extra cleaning looks responsible.

Extra research looks informed.

Extra supervision looks devoted.

Sometimes extra care is needed. A sick baby needs more monitoring than a well baby. A new medication requires attention. A changing developmental stage brings new hazards.

The question is whether the extra action responds to a real change or to the persistence of anxiety.

If nothing external changed and the only new evidence is "I still feel uncertain," the extra action deserves scrutiny.

An Ordinary-Safety Audit

Choose one trigger.

Write two headings.

Real rule

Describe the proportionate safety requirement from a reliable source or obvious condition.

OCD addition

Describe what you do beyond that rule to make anxiety settle.

Example:

Real rule: Fasten the car-seat harness according to the manufacturer's instructions before driving.

OCD addition: Pull every strap six times, photograph the buckle, and ask my partner to confirm the photo.

Now circle one OCD addition to reduce.

Do not alter the real rule.

If you are not confident that you can distinguish them, bring the example to your clinician.

A Note About Medical Uncertainty

Sometimes a baby has symptoms that are genuinely ambiguous.

Parents must decide whether to call a pediatrician.

OCD can make that process harder, but the answer is not to stop asking medical questions.

Create decision rules with the baby's clinician where possible.

"What symptoms should prompt a same-day call?"

"What symptoms are an emergency?"

"What can be monitored at home?"

"What reliable source should I use if I forget?"

Then use the plan.

Repeatedly asking the same question without new symptoms may be compulsive. New symptoms deserve new assessment.

The Goal Is Flexibility

An OCD-free life is not a life with zero rules.

It is a life in which rules fit the situation and can change when evidence changes.

You can follow a medical recommendation without turning it into a ritual.

You can be cautious when tired without concluding that all tiredness makes you dangerous.

You can ask for help because you need rest without turning the helper into a permanent supervisor.

You can notice an intrusive thought and continue the task.

Flexibility is a better marker than fearlessness.

Visitors and Family Rules

Infant safety discussions can become especially difficult when relatives have different standards.

A grandparent may do something you dislike.

A friend may arrive with a cold.

A family member may dismiss a rule you consider important.

Not every conflict is OCD.

Use the same sequence.

What does the reliable guidance say?

What is your household's reasonable rule?

What boundary follows?

Then notice whether OCD adds a demand that nobody ever make a mistake, disagree, or create uncertainty.

You are allowed to set ordinary parenting boundaries.

You do not have to turn every boundary into a ritualized inspection system.

When Two Reliable Sources Differ

Sometimes reputable guidance is not perfectly identical.

That can be hard for OCD.

Choose the source appropriate to your location and baby's care, or ask the treating pediatric clinician which recommendation to follow.

Then stop collecting sources solely to eliminate the discomfort of disagreement.

Medical guidance changes because evidence and systems differ. Your task is not to resolve every professional debate before you can parent.

A Rule Can Be Reasonable and Still Be Used Compulsively

Sometimes OCD does not invent a false safety rule. It repeats a real one.

Checking a buckle once is reasonable.

Checking it again and again because certainty will not arrive is compulsive use of a reasonable action.

Washing hands after a genuinely dirty task is reasonable.

Repeating the same wash until the internal feeling is correct can become compulsive.

This distinction prevents a common argument: "But the action itself is sensible."

The action may be sensible.

The repetition, function, and stopping rule are what changed.

When you discuss a ritual with a clinician, describe how many times it occurs and what makes you stop, not only what the action is called.

In a Nutshell

Everyday infant care contains real safety responsibilities, which is why harm OCD can hide inside "being careful."

Define the real rule first. Use reliable medical, pediatric, product, or public-health guidance where appropriate.

Then identify what OCD adds after the real rule is complete: repeated checking, avoidance, supervision, reassurance, emotional testing, or a private ritual.

Do not remove genuine safety measures for exposure.

Reduce the OCD-only layer gradually, especially when the distinction is hard.

The goal is not careless parenting. It is ordinary care without a second system built to eliminate every trace of uncertainty.

Chapter 12: Partners and Reassurance

Jordan's partner had learned the script without realizing it.

Jordan would say, "Do you think that thought means anything?"

The partner would say, "No. You love the baby. You would never do that."

Jordan would ask, "But are you sure?"

The partner would add evidence.

Jordan had always been gentle. Jordan was terrified by the thought. Jordan had been assessed for OCD. Jordan had never shown violent behavior.

Relief arrived.

An hour later, the script ran again.

Partners can become part of an OCD cycle because reassurance is an act of love with an unintended training effect. Reducing that reassurance does not require becoming cold. It requires changing the kind of help being offered.

Perinatal OCD consensus recommendations include partners and families as part of care because symptoms and treatment affect the household, not only the person with OCD (Mulcahy et al., 2023).

Support and Reassurance Are Not the Same

Support says, "I am with you while this is difficult."

Reassurance says, "I will answer the obsessional question until you feel certain."

Support can be practical.

"I will take the baby for an hour so you can sleep."

Support can be emotional.

"I can see this is hitting hard today."

Support can be treatment-oriented.

"Your plan is not to answer that question again. Do you want me to sit with you while you let it pass?"

None of these gives a moral guarantee.

The distinction can feel artificial at first. If certainty has been the main form of comfort, removing it may feel like removing care.

That is why partners need a replacement, not only a prohibition.

The Partner's First Fear

A partner who hears an infant-harm thought may be frightened too.

They deserve information and a chance to ask questions of the treating clinician when the patient consents and service rules allow.

The goal is not to tell the partner, "Do not worry, it is definitely nothing."

The goal is to explain the assessment.

"What makes the clinician think this is obsessional?"

"What signs would change the safety plan?"

"What compulsions should we avoid accommodating?"

"What should we do in an emergency?"

When both adults understand the formulation, the partner does not have to invent a risk system from scratch.

A Two-Sentence Response

Agree on a short response before the next reassurance request.

For example:

"I know the OCD question feels urgent. I am not going to give another certainty answer, but I can stay with you while you follow the plan."

Or:

"I care that you are distressed. If there is new safety information, tell me; if this is the same reassurance question, let's not feed it."

The exact wording matters less than consistency.

Do not make the response a lecture.

Long explanations can become elaborate reassurance.

The Emergency Exception

A reassurance boundary must never block genuine disclosure.

Agree on an exception:

"If you have new intent, a plan, psychotic symptoms, cannot maintain safety, or there has been an actual harmful event, tell me directly and we will get professional help."

This is not an invitation to reclassify every obsession as "new information."

The couple can ask the clinician what changes should trigger reassessment.

That makes the boundary safer and clearer.

Accommodation

Family accommodation occurs when relatives change behavior to reduce the person's OCD distress or help complete rituals.

In postpartum harm OCD, accommodation might include:

Always supervising routine infant care solely because of obsessional fear.

Taking over every diaper change.

Answering repeated reassurance questions.

Checking objects on the parent's behalf.

Participating in cleaning rituals.

Reading online material and reporting only reassuring passages.

Avoiding family activities because they trigger the person.

Some accommodation is hard to distinguish from ordinary support.

A partner may take over night care because the parent needs sleep. That is practical.

A partner may take over night care because the parent believes any intrusive thought means she must never be alone with the baby. If assessment identifies that rule as OCD-driven, it may become a treatment target.

Function again matters.

Do Not Remove Accommodation All at Once

A frustrated partner may hear "do not reassure" and stop everything overnight.

That can create conflict and may not match the treatment plan.

Better to choose one pattern.

Perhaps the couple begins with one reassurance question.

They agree that the partner will answer the first practical question if it is genuinely new, then use the two-sentence response for repeats.

Later they address a transferred care task.

ERP works best as planned learning rather than household punishment.

The person with OCD should know what is changing and why.

The Partner Is Not the Therapist

A partner can support ERP.

They should not design the entire treatment, police every compulsion, or decide risk alone.

That role strain can damage both people.

If the person with OCD asks, "Was that a compulsion?", the partner does not need to adjudicate every event.

A useful answer is, "Make a note and ask your therapist. I do not want to become the checker."

If symptoms are severe, the partner also needs a clear professional contact route.

The household should not depend on one exhausted adult to make every mental health decision.

Practical Support Is Treatment-Compatible

New parents need practical help whether or not OCD is present.

Meal preparation.

Laundry.

Transport.

Childcare for older children.

Protected sleep opportunities.

Attending appointments.

Handling insurance or referral calls.

These forms of support can increase a person's capacity to engage in treatment.

Do not confuse "stop accommodating OCD" with "stop helping."

If a parent is recovering from birth or severely sleep deprived, asking her to shoulder every task to prove she is not avoiding is not treatment.

Choose targets based on the OCD formulation, not on an ideology of independence.

When the Partner Needs Certainty Too

Sometimes the reassurance loop runs in both directions.

The parent says, "I had a thought."

The partner asks, "But you would tell me if it felt real, right?"

The parent reassures the partner.

The partner asks again.

Soon both people are checking.

This is understandable after taboo disclosure.

The solution is shared access to the clinical plan.

The partner can bring safety concerns to the clinician rather than using the person with OCD as the source of certainty.

If the partner notices genuinely new behavior, severe confusion, psychotic symptoms, a stated intent, or inability to care safely, they should act on that information.

If nothing has changed and the question is "Can you promise me forever?", the partner may need to tolerate uncertainty too.

What to Say After a Hard Thought

Try one of these:

"Do you want practical help, company, or help following the treatment plan?"

"That sounds painful. I will not analyze what it means with you."

"I remember the plan. We are not checking your character."

"Let's do the next ordinary task."

"I can listen to how hard the moment is without deciding the OCD question."

These lines keep the relationship human.

Do not recite them mechanically. Use your own voice.

What Not to Say

Some responses add shame.

"How could you think that?"

"Do not ever say that again."

"Just stop thinking about it."

"If you loved the baby, you would not have these thoughts."

Others feed certainty.

"I promise on my life that you are 100 percent safe."

"I have analyzed you and there is no possible risk."

"Tell me every detail so I can decide."

A partner does not need perfect language. Repair matters.

If you said something unhelpful, you can say, "I reacted because I was scared. I want us to use the clinical plan instead of guessing."

The Conversation About Childcare

OCD can distort who does what.

One parent may be carrying nearly all infant care because the other is avoiding.

Or the parent with OCD may be doing everything because she cannot trust anyone else to meet her rules.

Both patterns deserve attention.

List the main care tasks.

Feeding.

Diapering.

Bathing.

Bedtime.

Appointments.

Transport.

Household cleaning.

Then ask whether the current division reflects practical needs or OCD rules.

You do not need perfect equality.

You need a division that is sustainable and does not quietly train avoidance.

Partners and Disclosure to Clinicians

A support person can attend an appointment if the patient wants them there and the service allows it.

Beforehand, agree on the role.

The partner can share observed behavior.

"She checks the baby repeatedly."

"He has stopped using the kitchen."

"They ask me the same safety question many times."

The partner can report concerning changes.

"She has not slept despite having the opportunity and seems unusually energized."

"He said he has a plan to hurt himself."

The partner should not minimize because they fear hospitalization, nor exaggerate because the thought content frightened them.

Describe what happened.

Let the clinician assess.

Intimacy and Resentment

OCD treatment unfolds inside a relationship already changed by a baby.

There may be less time, more work, financial pressure, physical recovery, sexual changes, family conflict, and interrupted sleep.

Reassurance can become one more demand.

The partner may feel resentful.

The person with OCD may feel ashamed of needing help.

Neither feeling makes someone cruel.

Schedule one conversation about the household that is not held during an OCD spike.

Ask:

"What support is actually helping?"

"What reassurance pattern is exhausting us?"

"What task division needs to change?"

"What do we do when one of us thinks symptoms are getting worse?"

A ten-minute practical meeting can prevent every difficult moment from becoming a relationship referendum.

When There Is No Supportive Partner

Some readers are parenting alone.

Some have a partner who travels or works long hours.

Some are in relationships that are unsafe.

Some have partners who dismiss mental health symptoms.

Do not build recovery around a person who is not available.

Identify another support layer: a relative, friend, postpartum service, home visitor, therapist, primary-care clinician, support group, community resource, or paid help if accessible.

If there is domestic violence, coercive control, or fear of a partner, disclose that to an appropriate professional or specialist service. Couples work is not a substitute for safety planning in an abusive situation.

A Partner Plan

Write four lines together if possible.

When the same reassurance question appears: "We will use our two-sentence response."

When practical help is needed: "We will ask directly for the task, not wrap it in an OCD question."

When symptoms change: "We will contact the treating clinician."

When urgent signs appear: "We will use the emergency plan."

Keep the plan where both people can find it.

Do not turn it into a contract with penalties.

It is a shared cue.

The Role of Warmth

Some people fear that response prevention requires emotional distance.

It does not.

A partner can hug you without telling you what the thought means.

They can bring food without analyzing the obsession.

They can listen while you say, "This is a rough hour."

They can laugh with you about something unrelated.

They can take the baby so you can attend therapy.

Certainty is only one form of comfort, and in OCD it may be the least durable one.

A Planned Check-In

Some couples benefit from a short scheduled OCD check-in.

Ten or fifteen minutes.

Once a day or a few times a week.

The person with OCD can report treatment-relevant changes.

The partner can raise accommodation problems.

Both can decide what practical help is needed.

Then OCD does not need to occupy every conversation.

A scheduled check-in should not become a daily reassurance session. Keep the focus on behavior and plan changes.

"What did we do differently?"

"What support do we need?"

"What should go to the clinician?"

Avoid "Convince me again that I am safe."

When Partners Disagree About Risk

Do not settle a serious disagreement by arguing until one person gives in.

If one partner believes symptoms have changed in a way that affects safety and the other believes it is the same OCD pattern, bring the concern to an appropriate clinician.

If the concern is urgent, use urgent services.

The partner may be wrong.

The person with OCD may be wrong.

A professional assessment is safer than making the relationship carry the full burden of the decision.

Protecting the Relationship From Treatment Talk

Agree on at least one period in the day when OCD is not the default subject unless there is urgent information.

Eat.

Watch something.

Walk.

Talk about work, family, or the baby as a person rather than as a risk topic.

This is not suppression.

It is keeping the relationship larger than the disorder.

If One Partner Is Not Ready to Reduce Reassurance

The person with OCD may understand the treatment before the partner does.

A frightened partner may keep offering certainty because stopping feels cruel or unsafe.

Do not turn this into a private contest.

Invite the partner to one clinical conversation if possible.

Ask the therapist to explain the difference between support, accommodation, and new safety information.

Choose one reassurance pattern to change first.

The partner is learning too.

If they remain unable or unwilling to follow the plan, build other supports and tell the clinician. Treatment should not depend on winning every household disagreement.

If the Person With OCD Becomes Angry About the Boundary

A reassurance boundary can feel rejecting in the moment.

Name the difference.

"I am saying no to the certainty answer, not no to you."

Then offer something real.

A glass of water.

A practical task.

Company.

A scheduled treatment check-in.

Warmth and boundaries can occupy the same minute.

A Household Phrase for Repeated Questions

Couples often do better with a phrase that belongs to them.

"Same question."

"Old loop."

"Plan, not proof."

Choose something neutral.

The phrase should not become sarcasm or a way to shut down all mental health conversation. It means only that both people recognize a familiar reassurance pattern.

After the cue, the person with OCD decides the next step.

The partner can remain present without supplying another answer.

Principles to Remember

Partners can accidentally become part of the OCD cycle by providing repeated reassurance or changing family life around avoidance.

Reducing accommodation should be planned, gradual, and paired with other forms of support.

The partner is not the therapist or sole risk assessor. Shared access to the clinical plan matters.

A simple response can validate distress without answering the certainty question.

Practical help, rest, affection, and ordinary conversation remain available.

The household goal is not zero dependence. It is support that helps both people live rather than support that serves the compulsion.

Chapter 13: Bad Nights and No Sleep

At 2:17 a.m., Amara's baby finished a feed and settled.

Amara did not.

She had the opportunity to sleep for perhaps two hours. Instead, she reviewed a thought from earlier in the day. She searched for a phrase she had already searched. She checked whether her fear felt intense enough. When the baby woke again, Amara had spent the entire interval trying to decide whether she was safe.

Sleep loss did not create the obsession from nothing. It made every step harder.

The postpartum period is full of interrupted sleep, but "sleep deprived" can describe very different situations. One parent is exhausted because a newborn feeds often. Another cannot sleep even when someone else has the baby because anxiety and rumination keep her awake. Another sleeps very little yet feels unusually energized and develops rapid speech, grandiose beliefs, severe agitation, or psychotic symptoms.

Those patterns do not have the same meaning.

This chapter is about the ordinary collision between OCD and disrupted sleep. It also keeps one boundary clear: a marked reduction in need for sleep with mania, psychosis, severe confusion, or rapidly changing behavior needs urgent medical assessment. Postpartum psychosis can develop quickly and is a psychiatric emergency (Toor et al., 2024; NICE, 2014/2020).

Tired Minds Want Fast Certainty

When you are exhausted, a long treatment explanation is hard to use.

The mind asks a short question:

"Am I dangerous?"

You want a short answer:

"No."

That answer can produce relief, which makes reassurance especially attractive at night.

The difficulty is that certainty expires.

A tired brain may also have less patience for uncertainty. You may feel less able to tolerate an image, a strange sensation, or a question left open. Rumination can seem easier than sleeping because it feels like active prevention.

The practical answer is not to demand more mental discipline from an exhausted person. It is to simplify the response.

Nighttime is not the time to solve your identity.

A Night Rule

Create one rule before the next difficult night:

No new private diagnosis after bedtime.

That means you do not decide at 1:00 a.m. that an old obsession has suddenly proved you are dangerous because the fear feels sharper.

It does not mean ignoring new emergency symptoms.

If you develop actual intent, a plan, hallucinations, delusions, severe confusion, marked mania, or inability to maintain safety, use the urgent plan.

If it is the same obsessional question with no new safety information, postpone analysis until daytime and follow the treatment response you already chose.

You can write:

"Same question, same plan. I will discuss new information with my clinician tomorrow."

That is not reassurance. It is a decision about when not to conduct an investigation.

Night Searching

Phones make reassurance available at any hour.

A search can begin with one clinical question and end forty-five minutes later in a forum thread from seven years ago.

Night searching is especially sticky because there are fewer competing activities. The baby may be feeding. The house is quiet. You can scroll with one hand.

Build friction.

Keep the browser closed during feeds unless you need it for a practical task.

Move OCD bookmarks out of immediate reach.

Write the question in a note if you believe it may be clinically relevant.

Review the note in daylight before deciding whether to ask your clinician.

If the question still matters and has not already been answered, ask once.

If the question looks like the same reassurance loop, let it remain unanswered.

The goal is not digital purity. It is to stop turning every wake period into an OCD research session.

The Minimum Viable SAFE Return

On a rested day, the full SAFE Return may feel manageable.

At night, use the smallest version.

Spot: "OCD question."

Allow: "Not solving it now."

Forego: no search or review.

Engage: finish the feed, place the baby safely, and take the next chance to rest.

You do not need to feel convinced.

The point is to protect behavior from a tired mind's demand for a verdict.

When the Baby Is Crying and You Are Angry

Exhaustion can reduce patience.

A baby may cry despite feeding, rocking, changing, and every reasonable attempt to soothe.

You may feel anger.

You may think, "I cannot take this."

A harm image may arrive immediately.

First, use a real safety plan.

If you are overwhelmed, place the baby in a safe location according to current infant-care guidance and step away briefly, or hand the baby to another safe adult. If you fear you may act violently or cannot maintain safety, seek urgent help.

That practical action is not OCD avoidance. It is responding to actual behavioral overwhelm.

After the immediate situation settles, OCD may ask you to investigate the anger.

"How angry was I?"

"Would a good mother need a break?"

"Did I put the baby down too quickly?"

If there was no harmful act and no new safety concern, do not turn appropriate self-regulation into evidence for a moral trial.

Tell your clinician if anger or loss-of-control fears are frequent. A treatment plan can address both practical coping and obsessional interpretation.

Sleep Opportunity Matters

When a clinician asks how much you sleep, include whether you had a chance to sleep.

A parent waking every two hours for feeding and wishing desperately for more rest is describing infant-driven disruption.

A parent whose partner takes the baby for six hours but who remains awake ruminating is describing a different barrier.

A parent who sleeps very little despite opportunity and does not feel tired, while becoming markedly more energized or behaviorally changed, raises another concern.

These are not diagnostic formulas. They show why "I slept three hours" needs context.

If your symptoms include a striking loss of need for sleep, unusual energy, severe agitation, grandiose or fixed beliefs, hallucinations, or confusion, seek medical assessment promptly. NICE advises immediate specialist assessment for sudden symptoms suggesting postpartum psychosis (NICE, 2014/2020).

Protecting a Sleep Opportunity

If another safe adult can take over care for a planned period, decide in advance what you will not do with that time.

No reassurance searching.

No detailed symptom audit.

No rewriting the disclosure note.

No checking the baby's monitor outside the plan.

The purpose of the protected period is rest.

You may not fall asleep immediately. Rest can still include lying down, dimming stimulation, and letting the body be off duty. If insomnia persists, tell a clinician. Postpartum sleep difficulty can be both a symptom and a stressor, and persistent insomnia deserves assessment rather than endless self-management.

The Monitor Problem

Baby monitors can become checking devices.

A parent may watch normal movement for long stretches, zoom in repeatedly, or replay recordings.

If a monitor is part of your ordinary setup, decide how it is meant to be used.

What signal requires action?

When is checking appropriate?

What would a non-OCD household member reasonably do?

Then keep the stopping rule.

Do not use the monitor to obtain a feeling that the baby will remain safe for the rest of the night.

No monitor can provide that.

If your baby has a medical monitoring plan, follow the clinical instructions instead of a general rule from this book.

"I Am Worse at Night, So Maybe the Thought Is More Real"

Symptoms often feel different when people are tired.

A thought may feel louder.

Emotions may feel flatter.

Your concentration may be worse.

You may have less capacity to resist a ritual.

OCD can interpret the change as evidence: "The thought feels less upsetting tonight. Maybe I want it."

That creates emotional checking at the exact time your emotional system is depleted.

Do not grade a thought by how dramatic your reaction is at midnight.

Describe patterns to your clinician over time.

Then use the same response plan unless genuinely new information appears.

Feeding as a Compulsion Cue

Night feeds can become linked to a particular obsession simply through repetition.

The chair, bottle, breast pump, nursery, or darkness becomes a cue.

You may start dreading the feed before the thought appears.

That anticipatory fear can create avoidance or reassurance rituals.

Use the ordinary task as a planned practice when appropriate.

Before the feed:

"I may have the thought. I will not use the feed to test myself."

During:

Notice the thought and return to the practical steps of feeding.

After:

Do not conduct a review of whether you felt the right emotions.

If the feed itself has medical or lactation complications, address those with the relevant professional. Treatment should not turn genuine feeding problems into exposure material.

The 3:00 a.m. Promise

Avoid making large treatment promises during a spike.

"I will never ask for reassurance again."

"Tomorrow I will do the hardest exposure."

"I am deleting every app."

These promises can create a punishment cycle.

Morning arrives, the plan is unrealistic, and you conclude you failed.

Choose one small night rule that is possible:

No forum search during feeds.

One fewer monitor check.

No replay of the diaper change.

Write the clinical question down instead of sending five messages.

A modest plan repeated is more useful than a dramatic vow.

When a Partner Is Also Exhausted

A partner may respond badly at night because they are tired too.

They may reassure just to end the conversation.

They may snap.

They may say, "We already talked about this."

Prepare the response during daylight.

Agree on one phrase.

"Same OCD question. I care, and I am not answering it again."

Agree on practical support.

"After this feed, I will take the baby for ninety minutes."

Agree on emergency information.

"If you tell me you have new intent, a plan, psychotic symptoms, or cannot keep the baby safe, we act."

Night does not need a full relationship negotiation.

Single Parenting at Night

If you are the only adult in the home, a plan matters even more.

Identify who can be contacted for practical help.

Know the urgent-care route.

Ask clinicians what support exists locally.

Plan small ERP tasks that do not depend on a partner.

If symptoms are severe enough that you cannot safely manage infant care alone, tell your clinician. The solution may involve more support or a higher level of care, not a harder self-help challenge.

Lack of household support is a real constraint. It should be part of treatment planning.

A Bad Night Does Not Reset Treatment

Suppose you search for an hour after two weeks of progress.

The next morning OCD offers another all-or-nothing conclusion.

"You are back at the beginning."

No.

A compulsion happened.

Study the sequence briefly.

What was the trigger?

What made the ritual easier to start?

What small barrier can you add next time?

Then resume the plan.

Do not spend the next day reviewing why you "failed." That is the same mechanism in a different costume.

When Sleep Becomes a Medical Question

Talk with a medical or mental health professional when insomnia is persistent, worsening, or accompanied by significant mood symptoms.

Seek urgent assessment when sleep change occurs with symptoms suggesting psychosis or mania, severe confusion, rapidly changing behavior, suicidal or harmful intent, or inability to maintain safety.

Do not start sedating medication, change a psychiatric dose, or use another person's medication based on a book.

Medication and sleep decisions in pregnancy or breastfeeding need individual medical review.

A Night-Feed Plan

Write this in five lines.

Ordinary care: What does the baby need during this feed?

OCD cue: Which repeated question usually appears?

Response prevention: Which one ritual will I not do?

Practical support: What can another person do, if available?

Urgent exception: What symptoms mean I use the emergency plan?

Example:

Ordinary care: feed, burp, safe sleep placement.

OCD cue: "What if the image means I will act?"

Response prevention: no online search.

Practical support: partner takes the next feed.

Urgent exception: actual intent, plan, psychotic symptoms, severe confusion or mania, inability to maintain safety.

The plan should fit on one screen.

The Next-Day Reset

Morning after a bad night can produce a second problem: shame.

You may look at the search history, remember the reassurance questions, and decide the night proves treatment is failing.

Use a short reset.

First, meet basic needs that are possible: food, water, medication as prescribed, and a rest opportunity if one can be arranged.

Second, tell the clinician if the sleep change is significant or persistent.

Third, choose one ritual to handle differently that night.

Do not write a complete theory of why you struggled.

Fatigue is already a load. Recovery does not need an additional punishment task.

If You Are Afraid to Sleep

Some parents with harm OCD fear sleep itself.

They worry they will act while not fully awake, dream something disturbing, fail to hear the baby, or lose control.

The avoidance can produce more exhaustion, which makes the whole system harder.

Tell a clinician if fear is preventing sleep when opportunity exists. The treatment may include ERP for the sleep-related obsession, practical infant-care planning, or assessment for another sleep or mental health problem.

Do not keep yourself awake as a private safety measure without discussing it.

A Morning Question

After a difficult night, ask:

"What needs clinical attention, and what needs response prevention?"

A new severe symptom may need the clinician.

The same reassurance loop may need the treatment plan.

Separating those two tasks prevents you from treating every rough night as an emergency or every serious change as OCD.

A Daytime Sleep Conversation

Do not wait for the worst night to decide how sleep will be shared.

During the day, talk about what is realistically possible.

Which feed or care period can another adult cover?

What rest opportunity can be protected?

What happens if rumination uses that opportunity?

What symptoms should prompt a clinician call?

What happens if the partner is also depleted?

The plan may be imperfect because babies are unpredictable.

Even a loose plan is better than making every decision while both adults are exhausted.

If no other adult is available, tell your care team that sleep support is limited. That constraint belongs in the clinical picture.

Principles to Remember

Sleep disruption can intensify distress and make compulsions harder to resist, but one low-sleep night does not diagnose a psychiatric emergency.

Context matters. Include the opportunity to sleep, your level of tiredness, mood and energy changes, reality testing, and behavior when describing sleep to a clinician.

A marked reduction in need for sleep alongside mania, psychosis, severe confusion, or rapid behavioral change requires prompt assessment.

At night, use the smallest workable response. Do not conduct private diagnostic research during every wake period.

Protect sleep opportunities from OCD tasks where possible. Treat persistent insomnia as a clinical issue, not a moral failure.

Chapter 14: Medication and Perinatal Decisions

The medication question often arrives loaded with the same theme as the OCD.

"If I take something, what if it harms the baby?"

"If I do not take something, what if untreated OCD harms the baby?"

"What if I choose wrong?"

That structure is familiar: a high-responsibility decision, incomplete certainty, and a mind demanding a guarantee.

Medication decisions in pregnancy and breastfeeding are real medical decisions. They should not be reduced to an exposure exercise or settled by a general book.

This chapter gives you a way to prepare for the conversation.

For OCD in general, serotonin reuptake inhibitors, especially selective serotonin reuptake inhibitors called SSRIs, are established medication options. The International OCD Foundation lists SSRIs as first-line medications for OCD, and its perinatal OCD resources discuss SSRIs as a treatment option that may be used with ERP or when ERP is unavailable (International OCD Foundation, n.d.). Perinatal prescribing requires individual risk-benefit review that considers the specific medicine, dose, pregnancy stage, breastfeeding, symptom severity, prior treatment response, comorbidities, and the risks of untreated illness.

No universal paragraph can make that decision for you.

Medication Is Not a Moral Choice

Some parents interpret taking medication as evidence that they are weak.

Others interpret not taking it as evidence that they are reckless.

Neither frame helps.

Medication is a treatment option.

The clinical question is whether expected benefits and known or possible risks make sense for your situation, compared with alternatives and with the risks of leaving significant symptoms untreated.

That comparison can change over time.

A person with mild symptoms, good access to ERP, and strong function may make one choice with a prescriber.

A person with severe OCD who cannot eat, sleep, or complete infant care may make another.

A person who previously responded well to a particular medication may have information that changes the discussion.

The decision belongs in individualized care.

Do Not Stop Suddenly Because You Are Frightened

Pregnancy announcements can trigger abrupt medication decisions.

A parent reads a scary headline and stops a psychiatric medication that night.

Another parent sees a reassuring post and increases a dose without speaking to the prescriber.

Both are risky ways to manage a medical treatment.

Do not start, stop, or change psychiatric medication based on this book or a forum. Contact the prescriber.

If you discover a pregnancy while taking medication, tell the clinician what you take, the dose, how long you have taken it, what happens when you miss doses, and how well it has worked.

If the medicine cannot be reviewed immediately and you are worried, use an appropriate pharmacist, maternity service, primary-care clinician, or urgent service for guidance rather than improvising.

Why the Internet Makes This Harder

Medication information online often collapses complex evidence into a single word.

"Safe."

"Dangerous."

"Natural."

"Toxic."

Perinatal evidence rarely fits those categories cleanly.

Research may come from observational studies because randomized medication trials in pregnancy have ethical and practical limits. Underlying illness can complicate comparisons. Different medicines have different evidence. Timing and dose matter. Breastfeeding exposure differs from pregnancy exposure. A rare risk can sound enormous when presented without baseline context.

A prescriber who works with perinatal patients can explain what is known, what remains uncertain, and how the evidence applies to your history.

You do not need to become a pharmacologist.

You need to ask questions that produce a decision you can live with without conducting endless private research.

Five Questions for the Prescriber

Write these down.

One: What are we treating, and how severe is it right now?

A medication decision should be tied to a clinical target.

Two: What are the known benefits and risks of this specific medication in pregnancy or breastfeeding, and how certain is the evidence?

Ask for absolute risks where available, not only relative language.

Three: What are the risks of leaving my current symptoms untreated or undertreated?

Doing nothing is also a clinical option with consequences.

Four: What alternatives do we have, including ERP, a different medication, dose adjustment, timing, or closer monitoring?

The menu may depend on your history.

Five: What changes should make me contact you urgently, and what follow-up will we use?

A plan reduces late-night improvisation.

Prior Response Is Useful Information

If you took medication before pregnancy, bring the history.

What was the medicine?

What dose?

How long did you take it?

Did it reduce obsessions or compulsions?

What side effects occurred?

What happened when you stopped?

Did another medication fail?

Previous treatment response is one part of the clinical history a prescriber can use when individualizing perinatal mental health treatment (American College of Obstetricians and Gynecologists, 2023).

The best medicine on a generic list may not be the best choice for your history.

SSRIs and OCD

SSRIs are often known as antidepressants, but they are also used to treat OCD. The IOCDF identifies SSRIs as first-line medication treatments for OCD and notes that OCD treatment may differ from depression in dose and duration (International OCD Foundation, n.d.).

That fact belongs in a book about harm OCD because a reader may otherwise reject an OCD prescription after seeing "antidepressant" on the label.

Do not use it to infer what dose you need.

OCD medication dosing is a prescriber decision, especially in the perinatal period.

If a clinician unfamiliar with OCD prescribes, it can be reasonable to ask how the plan accounts for OCD rather than depression alone.

Pregnancy: Risk-Benefit, Not Zero-Risk

No pregnancy is risk-free.

No untreated illness is consequence-free.

No medication decision has perfect information.

A perinatal medication conversation compares options under uncertainty.

The prescriber may discuss the medicine's pregnancy data, congenital-malformation findings, obstetric outcomes, neonatal adaptation, maternal side effects, relapse risk, and what is known about the underlying condition.

You may hear a risk described as "small" or "rare." Ask for numbers when reliable estimates exist.

"What is the baseline risk?"

"What is the estimated risk with this medicine?"

"How strong is the evidence?"

Those questions are better than searching until you find a page that feels safe.

Breastfeeding Is a Separate Question

A medicine's pregnancy evidence does not automatically answer breastfeeding.

Transfer into breast milk differs by drug.

Infant age, prematurity, health, dose, and feeding pattern may matter.

The prescriber may coordinate with the baby's pediatric clinician or a pharmacist with perinatal expertise.

Ask about what infant signs, if any, should be monitored.

Do not assume that "present in milk" means "clinically harmful," and do not assume that a low milk level means no monitoring is ever needed. The specific medicine matters.

Use evidence specific to the situation.

Medication and ERP

Medication and ERP are not rival camps.

Some people use ERP without medication.

Some use medication because symptoms are too severe to engage well in ERP.

Some use both.

The International OCD Foundation describes medication as a first-line OCD option and ERP as a first-line psychological treatment (International OCD Foundation, n.d.).

Your clinician can help decide sequence and combination.

The important point for this book is that medication should not become a substitute for learning how to respond differently to obsessions if compulsions remain a central problem. Likewise, ERP should not become a reason to refuse a medication discussion when symptoms are severe.

Side-Effect Checking

OCD can attach to medication once it starts.

You swallow a tablet.

You monitor every sensation.

A headache appears.

You search whether it means toxicity.

You look at the baby and inspect behavior.

You repeat the search.

Medication side effects deserve attention. Compulsive monitoring can still occur around real treatment.

Ask the prescriber in advance:

"Which common effects should I expect?"

"Which symptoms should prompt a routine call?"

"Which are urgent?"

"What should I not monitor repeatedly?"

Then follow the plan.

If a new symptom is severe or concerning, seek medical advice. Response prevention does not mean ignoring possible adverse effects.

Reproductive Safety Reassurance Can Become a Ritual

A clinician explains the evidence.

You feel better.

Two hours later, you find a different study.

You ask for another explanation.

Then another.

At some point, informed consent can become certainty seeking.

Agree on trusted sources.

Decide who makes the medical interpretation.

Set a limit on new research unless a new decision or symptom arises.

You can say, "I have enough information for this decision, even though no one can give me zero uncertainty."

That sentence is not saying the medicine is safe in every sense.

It is acknowledging how medical decisions actually work.

If You Are Afraid the Prescriber Will Dismiss OCD

Bring the symptom pattern.

"I have unwanted intrusive harm images and spend two to three hours a day checking, avoiding, and asking for reassurance."

Tell them what treatment you are receiving.

If the prescriber is not comfortable managing OCD, ask whether consultation with psychiatry or a perinatal mental health specialist is appropriate.

A medication visit should not require you to teach the entire disorder while distressed.

If Medication Is Not Accessible

Cost, insurance, location, wait lists, pregnancy status, breastfeeding preferences, prior side effects, or health conditions may limit options.

Ask what evidence-based psychological care is available.

Ask whether telehealth ERP is legal and available where you live.

Ask whether there are stepped-care or public mental health services.

Ask whether your maternity team can refer to a specialist.

Do not assume "no medication" means "no treatment."

Likewise, if ERP access is poor, tell the prescriber. That constraint belongs in the decision.

Tapering and Discontinuation

There may be times when you and the prescriber decide to reduce or stop medication.

Plan it.

Ask how quickly.

Ask what withdrawal or discontinuation symptoms can occur.

Ask how relapse will be monitored.

Ask what to do if symptoms return.

Do not make tapering a test of whether you are "really recovered."

Some people need longer treatment than others. Duration depends on history, recurrence, severity, response, and clinical judgment.

Planning for Future Pregnancies

If you have experienced perinatal OCD once, future family planning may bring fear.

You can use the history instead of treating it only as a threat.

Before another pregnancy, if possible, discuss:

What symptoms appeared first last time?

Which treatment helped?

Which medication decisions were difficult?

What sleep and support plans are realistic?

Which clinician will monitor symptoms?

What are the urgent signs?

A relapse-prevention plan cannot guarantee a symptom-free pregnancy.

It can reduce confusion if symptoms return.

A Prescriber Appointment Sheet

Write one page.

Current pregnancy or postpartum stage.

Breastfeeding status, if relevant.

Current symptoms and functional impact.

Current and past psychiatric diagnoses.

Medication history and response.

Current medicines, supplements, allergies, and relevant medical conditions.

ERP or therapy status.

Five questions from this chapter.

Do not edit the sheet to prove that you deserve or do not deserve medication.

It is a clinical summary.

A Note on Emergency Medication Decisions

If you are experiencing postpartum psychosis, severe mania, suicidality, harmful intent, or another acute psychiatric emergency, urgent treatment may involve medication decisions that are different from routine outpatient OCD care.

Do not delay emergency assessment because you are trying to settle pregnancy or breastfeeding questions privately.

In an emergency, tell clinicians that you are pregnant or breastfeeding and list current medications. Let the treating team weigh immediate safety and medical factors.

Values and Medication

Some readers want to make medication decisions based on a value such as protecting the baby.

That value can point in more than one direction.

Treatment may reduce severe symptoms that are impairing care.

Medication may carry risks or side effects that need consideration.

Avoiding all medication may fit one person's situation and be a poor choice in another.

Values do not erase evidence.

A good decision brings values and evidence into the same conversation.

Bring the Prescriber the OCD Pattern, Not Only the Anxiety

Medication visits can become vague when the patient says only, "I feel anxious."

Describe the target symptoms.

"Unwanted harm images."

"Two hours of rumination."

"Repeated reassurance."

"Avoiding infant care."

This helps the prescriber understand what change would count as improvement.

If treatment reduces general anxiety but compulsions remain severe, say so.

If intrusive thoughts remain but you are functioning better and ritualizing less, say that too.

Medication response should be judged against the clinical target, not a demand for a perfectly quiet mind.

Decisions During Breastfeeding Changes

Weaning, changing feeding frequency, returning to work, or a baby's medical change can alter the context in which medication questions are considered.

Do not assume an old answer automatically applies to a new circumstance.

Ask the prescriber or pharmacist when the situation changes materially.

Then avoid reopening the entire decision every day when nothing has changed.

What to Do With a Frightening Study

If you encounter research that worries you, save the citation once.

Do not read twenty interpretations.

Bring the paper or question to the prescriber:

"Does this study change the risk-benefit assessment for my medication and my situation?"

Let the clinician explain study design, relevance, and limits.

One frightening headline should not become a self-directed medication change.

The Decision Can Be Revisited Without Being Reopened Daily

A medication decision is not irreversible merely because you stop researching it tonight.

You can make a plan with the prescriber and set a review date.

At the review, examine symptoms, side effects, pregnancy or breastfeeding changes, adherence, and functioning.

Between reviews, contact the clinician sooner if a significant problem arises.

This structure gives medical decisions a legitimate reopening point.

OCD loses the argument that you must keep the case open every hour "just in case."

A scheduled review is not certainty. It is responsible follow-up.

Keep Medication Adherence Separate From Exposure

Do not skip, delay, or alter prescribed medication as an OCD exposure unless the prescribing clinician has explicitly directed a medication change.

Medication adherence is a medical task.

ERP should target the compulsive behavior around the medication, such as repeated label checking, internet searching, or reassurance, while the prescribed regimen remains intact.

If you are worried about the medicine, contact the prescriber.

Do not use uncertainty practice to improvise dosing.

In a Nutshell

Medication for perinatal OCD is an individualized medical decision. SSRIs are established first-line medication options for OCD, and ERP is a first-line psychological treatment, but pregnancy and breastfeeding require person-specific review.

Do not start, stop, or change psychiatric medication based on a book, a social-media post, or one frightening headline.

Bring your symptom severity, treatment history, prior medication response, pregnancy or breastfeeding context, and questions to a qualified prescriber.

Ask about the risks of treatment and the risks of undertreatment.

If OCD turns medication research into endless reassurance seeking, agree on trusted sources and a stopping rule with the clinician.

The goal is not a zero-uncertainty decision. It is an informed one.

Chapter 15: Bonding Without Checking

Elena had expected to look at her baby and feel something unmistakable.

Instead, she felt tired.

Then she felt afraid of feeling tired.

She held the baby and searched for warmth. When warmth came, she relaxed. When it did not, she wondered what was wrong with her. A few days later, a harm image appeared during a feeding. Now every cuddle had two tasks: care for the baby and prove that the relationship was safe.

The second task made the first almost impossible to experience naturally.

Bonding can become an OCD test when a parent treats every emotion as evidence. The treatment direction is not to manufacture the correct feeling. It is to stop using feeling as a moment-by-moment safety exam.

Bonding Is Not a Single Moment

Popular stories often portray bonding as immediate recognition.

Real relationships are more varied.

Some parents feel intense love quickly.

Some feel protective but emotionally flat.

Some feel relief, fear, grief, confusion, or unfamiliarity.

Some are recovering from a difficult birth, managing pain, feeding problems, depression, anxiety, trauma symptoms, or a medical complication.

The parent-infant relationship is built across repeated care, not decided by one emotional snapshot.

For a reader with OCD, that matters because the mind may search for a single verdict.

"Did I feel enough love during that feed?"

There is no useful threshold.

The repeated measurement can become the problem.

The Love Test

Maya's test had three parts.

Look at the baby.

Notice the first emotion.

Decide whether it is "motherly enough."

If the emotion was neutral, she tried again.

That repetition changed the experience. Instead of relating to the baby, Maya related to a measurement.

The response prevention was small.

Hold the baby.

Do not ask the feeling question.

Complete the care task.

If tenderness arrived, let it arrive.

If boredom arrived, let boredom be there.

If anxiety arrived, do not use it as a verdict.

The relationship does not require a performance review every five minutes.

When Numbness Feels Dangerous

Emotional numbness can be frightening.

It can occur with exhaustion, depression, trauma responses, anxiety, medication effects, physical illness, or other conditions. It deserves attention when persistent or distressing.

OCD can add a second interpretation:

"If I feel numb, maybe I could hurt the baby."

That leap is not a clinical assessment.

Tell your clinician about persistent numbness, low mood, loss of pleasure, detachment, or difficulty functioning. Let them assess depression, trauma, OCD, and other possibilities.

Then, if the numbness has become an OCD cue, practice caring behavior without checking whether the feeling has changed.

You do not have to feel warm before you can warm a bottle.

Irritation Does Not Cancel Care

A baby can be difficult to soothe.

A parent can be irritated.

Both can be true in a loving relationship.

OCD may insist that irritation is evidence of hidden intent, especially if a harm thought appears in the same moment.

Use behavior as the first safety guide.

If you are overwhelmed to the point that you fear losing control, put the baby in a safe place, step away briefly, involve another safe adult, and seek help as needed. If you have intent to harm or cannot maintain safety, use urgent services.

If the problem is an unwanted obsession following ordinary frustration, stop checking the emotion for moral meaning.

You can say, "I was frustrated and had an intrusive thought. I am going to follow the care plan."

No character trial is required.

Grief for the Postpartum Period You Expected

OCD can steal time.

You may have imagined stroller walks and instead spent the first months avoiding outside routes.

You may have imagined enjoying feeds and instead reviewed your mind through them.

You may look at photos and remember how frightened you were.

Grief about that loss is not a compulsion by itself.

The danger is turning grief into a demand to recover the past perfectly.

"I must enjoy every remaining week."

"I must make up for the days I was anxious."

"I must create enough good memories to cancel the bad ones."

Now the postpartum period becomes another performance.

Let the lost time be lost.

Recovery can begin from the day you are in.

Values-Led Care

Values answer a practical question:

"What kind of action matters here?"

Feed the baby.

Attend the appointment.

Read the story.

Ask a partner for rest.

Take the baby outside.

Complete the diaper change.

Hold the baby for comfort.

The action can be caring even when your mind is noisy.

A values-led life is not one in which you always feel your values vividly. It is one in which behavior can express them without waiting for emotional certainty.

This is particularly useful for harm OCD because the obsession often says, "Prove how you feel before you act."

Values reverse the order.

Act according to what matters.

Let feelings move on their own schedule.

The Trap of Photograph Evidence

Some parents use photos or videos to check bonding.

"Look how I was smiling. That proves I love the baby."

The image gives relief.

Later, OCD notices another photo where the parent looks tired.

Now the evidence conflicts.

You do not need to ban photos.

Use them as memories, not diagnostic records.

If you catch yourself searching the camera roll for proof of attachment, close it and return to current behavior.

A relationship is not a facial-expression dataset.

Comparing Yourself With Other Mothers

Social media offers endless comparison.

Another mother writes that she cried with joy at birth.

Someone posts that breastfeeding felt sacred.

Someone else says she misses her baby after thirty minutes apart.

OCD can turn those stories into standards.

"I did not cry."

"I felt relieved when someone took the baby."

"I enjoy time alone."

"Maybe I am different in a dangerous way."

Comparison selects a few visible moments from another person's life and uses them as evidence against your entire internal experience.

Reduce the comparison if it is operating as checking.

Unfollow accounts that become compulsive test material.

Not because other parents are wrong.

Because you are using their stories for a purpose they cannot serve.

When Depression Is Also Present

Low mood after birth deserves direct attention.

Depression can involve persistent sadness, loss of interest or pleasure, guilt, hopelessness, appetite or sleep changes, poor concentration, and suicidal thoughts. Symptoms in the perinatal period should be assessed by a qualified clinician.

OCD and depression can coexist (Hudepohl et al., 2022).

Do not interpret every loss of pleasure as evidence for a harm obsession.

Tell the clinician about both.

If you have suicidal intent or cannot stay safe, seek urgent help.

Treatment may need to address more than one condition.

When Trauma Is Also Present

A frightening birth, medical emergency, or earlier trauma can affect how a parent experiences the postpartum period.

Intrusive memories related to trauma differ from OCD obsessions in important ways, though symptoms can overlap and both can occur.

Do not force every unwanted image into one category.

Describe whether the image is a replay of an event, a feared future event, an obsessional possibility, or something you cannot classify.

A clinician can decide whether trauma-focused treatment, OCD treatment, or a combination is appropriate.

Physical Affection as Exposure

If OCD has made you avoid ordinary affectionate contact, a therapist may include it in a graded plan.

The target is not "feel love."

The target might be "hold the baby for five minutes without checking my internal state."

Or "kiss the baby's head without replaying whether it felt right."

Or "sit beside the baby during play without searching for proof of connection."

These are ordinary acts returned to ordinary status.

Do not repeat them to test whether the emotion changed.

When the Baby Does Not Respond as Expected

Babies are not exposure props.

They have temperaments, moods, developmental changes, and preferences.

A baby may turn away.

Cry when held.

Settle faster with another caregiver.

Refuse a feed.

Smile at a stranger.

OCD can interpret ordinary infant behavior as a verdict on bonding.

"The baby knows something is wrong with me."

That conclusion goes far beyond the observation.

Respond to the baby's practical need.

If feeding or development raises a genuine clinical concern, consult the appropriate professional.

Do not use every fussy moment as evidence about your identity.

Repair Is Part of Parenting

No parent responds perfectly.

You may misread a cue.

Become impatient.

Need to put the baby down.

Ask for help late.

Miss the calm response you hoped to give.

Repair is more useful than perfection.

Notice what happened.

Correct what can be corrected.

Apologize to a partner when needed.

Adjust the plan.

Then stop.

OCD wants repair to become penance.

It wants you to replay the mistake until you feel pure.

That is not required for learning.

A Seven-Day Bonding Experiment

For one week, choose one small care or connection action each day.

Do not choose based on how loving it feels.

Examples:

Read one short book aloud.

Sit on the floor during play.

Complete one feed without emotional checking.

Take a stroller walk.

Sing one song.

Do the bedtime routine.

Accept help and rest so you can return with more capacity.

After the action, record only:

"Done."

Do not rate love.

Do not rate anxiety.

Do not compare days.

At the end of the week, notice what happens when behavior is allowed to stand without emotional scoring.

What If I Do Not Enjoy Motherhood Right Now?

Then that is information, not a confession.

You may be exhausted.

You may have OCD.

You may have depression.

You may dislike the newborn stage.

You may be in pain.

You may love your child and dislike much of the work.

You may need more support.

You do not have to convert every honest feeling into a threat assessment.

Tell relevant clinicians about persistent low mood, detachment, hopelessness, or inability to function.

Then let personal preference remain personal.

Not enjoying every stage of parenting does not need an OCD interpretation.

The SAFE Return for Emotional Checking

Spot: "I am checking whether I feel the right thing."

Allow: "I may feel warm, numb, irritated, or uncertain."

Forego: no second cuddle for proof, no photo review, no partner question.

Engage: complete the care action you chose.

This is one of the quietest uses of the method.

Nobody else may know you are practicing.

Let the Baby Be a Person, Not a Test

OCD can make every interaction about you.

Did I smile correctly?

Did I feel enough?

Did I respond fast enough?

The baby disappears behind the measurement.

Try shifting attention outward without using distraction to erase the thought.

What sound is the baby making?

What are they looking at?

Are they hungry, tired, comfortable, or interested?

What practical response fits?

This moves the interaction back toward relationship.

You may still feel anxious.

The difference is that the baby's actual cue, not your internal score, directs the next action.

The Parent-Baby Relationship Can Include Help

Some parents with OCD believe that asking another adult to soothe the baby proves a weak bond.

That belief can create overfunctioning.

Healthy caregiving can involve multiple safe adults.

Accepting help because you need rest or because another person is available is not the same as transferring every task because an obsession says you are dangerous.

Ask about function.

"Am I sharing care, or am I escaping a feared test?"

Either answer can guide the next conversation with your clinician.

When Bonding Worries Need More Than OCD Work

If you feel persistently detached, hopeless, unable to experience pleasure, frightened of the baby in a way that is not explained by obsessions, or unable to engage in basic care, tell a professional.

Parent-infant relationship services, depression treatment, trauma treatment, feeding support, or other care may be relevant depending on the cause.

Do not force every relationship difficulty through one OCD method.

The wider picture still matters.

When Other People Comment on the Bond

Relatives may say, "She only settles for you," or, "He is such a daddy's boy," or, "You two are inseparable."

Positive comments can become reassurance.

Negative or careless comments can become evidence.

Try not to use either as a diagnostic statement.

A baby may settle differently with different people for many ordinary reasons.

If a professional who actually assesses parent-infant interaction raises a concern, discuss it.

If a relative makes an offhand remark, you do not need to conduct a week of emotional testing.

Returning to Pleasure Without Chasing It

As symptoms improve, you may notice enjoyable moments again.

Let them be enjoyable.

Do not grab the moment and ask, "Is this proof I am recovered?"

That question pulls you out of the experience and back into measurement.

Pleasure is allowed to arrive without becoming evidence.

So is an ordinary flat moment the next day.

A Behavioral Bonding Record

If you need a reminder of progress, record actions rather than feelings for one week.

"Read a book."

"Completed bath."

"Asked for help before overload."

"Attended pediatric appointment."

"Rested while partner cared for baby."

This record does not prove love.

It shows where your behavior is becoming more flexible and sustainable.

That is a treatment-relevant measure.

Ordinary Separation Can Be Part of the Relationship

Returning to work, leaving the baby with childcare, taking a shower while someone else watches the baby, or spending an hour with a friend can trigger bonding fears.

OCD may say distance proves indifference.

Another version says that enjoying the separation proves you wanted escape from the baby.

Neither conclusion follows automatically.

Use the practical question.

Is the baby with a safe caregiver?

Is the separation reasonable for your circumstances?

What do you need to do during that time?

Then let the emotional response vary.

You may miss the baby.

You may enjoy quiet.

You may feel both.

Do not turn the return home into a test of whether reunion feels intense enough.

When Care Feels Mechanical

Some days parenting is repetitive.

Feed.

Change.

Wash.

Settle.

Repeat.

OCD can interpret routine as emotional absence.

But care does not lose its value because it feels ordinary.

A meal prepared without a rush of tenderness still feeds the baby.

A diaper changed while thinking about tomorrow still protects comfort and health.

A parent does not need a special feeling attached to every task for the task to count as care.

In a Nutshell

Bonding is not decided by one feeling or one moment.

OCD can turn love, tenderness, disgust, numbness, anger, and even facial expressions into evidence.

Persistent low mood or numbness deserves clinical assessment because depression, trauma, physical illness, and other conditions can coexist with OCD.

For obsessional checking, shift the measure from emotion to behavior.

Choose ordinary care and connection actions without grading how they feel.

A relationship can grow while your internal state remains imperfect.

Chapter 16: When the Theme Changes

Three months after treatment began, Priya stopped avoiding the stairs.

She could carry the baby upstairs, notice a fall image, and continue without reviewing it.

Then the obsession changed.

During diapering, an unwanted sexual thought appeared.

Priya felt as if every week of progress had been fake.

"This is worse," she told herself. "The first theme must have been OCD, but this one says something real."

That sentence is a common trick of a changing obsession.

The content changes.

The mechanism asks the same old question: *Will you solve me before you live?*

New Theme, Old Structure

A theme can move from accidental harm to intentional harm.

From harm to contamination.

From contamination to sexual content.

From the baby to the partner.

From physical safety to bonding.

From "What if I hurt someone?" to "What if I am the kind of person who could?"

The new content feels uniquely important because it has not yet become familiar.

Look underneath.

Is the thought unwanted?

Does it create a demand for certainty?

Do you check, avoid, reassure, confess, research, or review?

Does relief last briefly?

If the loop is the same, the treatment principles may still apply.

That does not mean every new symptom is automatically OCD. New intent, psychotic symptoms, severe mood change, or other significant changes still require assessment.

Use pattern recognition without turning it into a blanket explanation.

The "This One Is Different" Effect

OCD can accept every previous lesson while making one exception.

"Yes, violent images can be intrusive. But this image felt calmer."

"Yes, bodily sensations can be ambiguous. But this sensation was stronger."

"Yes, reassurance can be a compulsion. But I need to ask about this exact variation."

The exception is the hook.

If your clinician has already assessed the theme and no clinically relevant information has changed, consider whether "this one is different" is asking for another certainty round.

You can bring new content to treatment without demanding a new verdict every time.

"Same mechanism, new costume" can be a useful note.

Say it once.

Then return to response prevention.

Sexual-Harm Themes

Sexual-harm obsessions may be especially difficult because people fear stigma, legal consequences, and what bodily sensation could mean.

The shame can produce extreme avoidance and confession.

Perinatal OCD resources explicitly recognize unwanted sexual and violent thoughts about the baby as possible obsessional content (Royal College of Psychiatrists, n.d.).

That does not mean all sexual thoughts involving a child are OCD.

Clinical assessment must distinguish unwanted obsessional thoughts from sexual interest, intent, behavior, psychosis, and other conditions.

If the theme is new, tell your clinician.

If it has already been assessed as OCD, treatment may include reducing body checking, emotional testing, repeated confession, and avoidance of ordinary care.

Do not search for graphic comparison stories.

The mechanism can be treated without collecting details from strangers.

Contamination Themes

A parent whose violent theme improves may begin worrying about germs, chemicals, food safety, or medication residue.

Some contamination precautions are real.

The OCD layer appears when the standard becomes impossible.

Hands are washed again because clean does not feel clean.

A bottle is discarded despite following the preparation rule.

Visitors are excluded beyond medical advice.

Laundry is repeated.

The parent seeks endless updates about rare pathogens.

Return to the ordinary-safety method.

Define the real rule.

Follow it.

Remove the extra ritual.

Health and Medical Themes

Babies get rashes, coughs, fevers, digestive changes, and other symptoms that sometimes need medical attention.

A parent with OCD may struggle to know when to call.

This is one area where pre-agreed thresholds help.

Ask the baby's clinician what symptoms are urgent, what needs a routine appointment, and what can be monitored.

Then use that guidance.

OCD may still say, "But what if the guideline misses the one rare case?"

That is the uncertainty layer.

Do not let response prevention stop you from seeking care for genuinely new or concerning symptoms. The goal is proportionate use of medical care, not underuse.

Relationship and Identity Themes

After birth, some people become obsessed with whether they love their partner, whether the relationship is right, whether parenthood changed their identity, or whether an unwanted thought reveals something about sexual orientation or character.

A book focused on perinatal harm OCD cannot treat every OCD theme fully.

The important transfer is this:

Content can change while compulsive certainty seeking remains recognizable.

If you begin spending hours checking attraction, love, memory, or identity, tell your OCD clinician.

Do not assume a new subject means you need an entirely different mental strategy.

Relapse Versus a Bad Day

A bad day is not automatically relapse.

A week with more intrusive thoughts is not automatically relapse.

Recovery is uneven.

A more useful relapse marker is behavior.

Are rituals increasing?

Is avoidance returning?

Are you seeking reassurance more often?

Are you hiding symptoms again?

Are ordinary care tasks shrinking?

Are you abandoning treatment appointments?

Those changes matter because they show the cycle regaining control.

Thought count alone can be misleading.

Some people experience intrusive thoughts throughout recovery but respond to them differently.

The Three Early Signs

Choose three signs that your OCD is getting more control.

Make them behavioral.

"Searching reassurance forums after midnight."

"Asking my partner to supervise diaper changes."

"Spending more than fifteen minutes reviewing a thought."

"Canceling therapy because I am ashamed of a new theme."

"Checking the baby's breathing beyond the agreed plan."

Behavioral signs are actionable.

"Feeling weird" is harder to use.

The Three Early Responses

Match each sign with a response.

If searching returns: block the usual route and tell the therapist.

If avoidance returns: resume the last workable exposure step.

If reassurance rises: restore the partner script.

If shame is making you hide a new theme: write the content and bring it to the appointment.

If medication adherence changes: contact the prescriber rather than self-adjusting.

Keep the responses small enough to use early.

A relapse plan should not wait until symptoms are severe.

Booster ERP

Some people benefit from booster sessions after formal treatment becomes less frequent.

The purpose is to refresh the formulation, update the hierarchy, and address new compulsions.

If a new postpartum stage creates new triggers, the old plan may need adjustment.

Returning to treatment is not evidence that the first treatment failed.

Skills need updating when circumstances change.

Ask your therapist at discharge or step-down:

"What early signs should bring me back?"

"How do I book a booster?"

"What if the obsession changes theme?"

"What should make me seek urgent rather than routine care?"

The Difference Between a Theme Shift and a Clinical Change

A theme shift changes the subject of an obsession.

A clinical change may alter the type or urgency of care.

Examples of clinical change include new hallucinations, fixed delusional beliefs, marked mania, severe confusion, actual intent or planning, a suicide crisis, inability to care safely, severe depression, major substance use, or a significant medical change.

Do not label these as "just a new OCD theme" without assessment.

The SAFE Return is not for dismissing new red flags.

When the mental state changes in a way that affects reality testing or safety, seek professional review.

The Anniversary Effect

A baby's developmental milestones can bring new triggers.

Starting solid food.

Rolling.

Crawling.

Bathing differently.

Changing car seats.

Returning to work.

Childcare.

New independence creates new possible mistakes, and OCD may treat each stage as a fresh risk environment.

Expecting new triggers can prevent surprise from being interpreted as failure.

You do not need to predict the exact content.

You need to recognize the response choice.

Real rule.

OCD addition.

SAFE Return.

Professional help when needed.

Returning to Work or Childcare

Leaving the baby with another caregiver can produce a different OCD pattern.

Some parents fear the caregiver will harm the baby.

Others fear they will cause harm by choosing the wrong caregiver.

Some fear the baby will bond "too much" with someone else.

Others check childcare updates constantly.

There are genuine decisions in childcare selection. Use ordinary due diligence.

Once you have made the decision, watch for repetitive checking that no new information justifies.

If you cannot work because reassurance monitoring takes over the day, bring that functional impact to treatment.

Future Pregnancies

A later pregnancy may reactivate old fears.

The mind may say, "Last time was terrible, so it will happen again."

History is relevant without being destiny.

Use the information.

Tell maternity and mental health clinicians early.

Review what helped.

Decide how medication will be handled if relevant.

Build a sleep and support plan.

Know the signs that previously marked worsening.

Arrange faster access to ERP if possible.

Preparation is different from compulsive prevention.

Preparation has a stopping point.

Recovery Is Not a Quiet Mind

This point deserves a final pass.

If your definition of recovery is "I never have an intrusive thought again," then one unwanted image can erase a year of work.

Use a behavioral definition instead.

Recovery means more freedom to do ordinary, valued activities with less compulsive control, even if intrusive thoughts sometimes occur.

You may still notice an image while carrying your baby.

You may still have a strange thought during diapering.

You may still dislike the thought.

The difference is that the thought no longer automatically buys an hour of your day.

That is a large change.

A Relapse Card

Write this on one page.

My three early signs:

Choose behavioral signs.

My three first responses:

Choose small actions.

My two people or services to contact:

A clinician, partner, friend, perinatal service, or other appropriate support.

My urgent signs:

Actual harmful intent or plan, psychotic symptoms, severe confusion or mania, inability to maintain safety, suicidal crisis, or another change your clinician tells you requires urgent care.

My reminder:

"New content does not require a new private trial."

Keep the card.

Do not reread it compulsively.

Use it when behavior shows the plan is needed.

The Urge to Start From Page One Again

A new theme can make you want to reread every explanation in the book.

Once may be useful.

Repeated rereading until the new theme feels safe is another reassurance route.

Ask what you actually forgot.

If you remember the mechanism and the urgent-care distinction, you probably do not need a fresh diagnosis from every chapter.

Bring the new theme to your clinician.

Apply the existing plan where appropriate.

Let novelty feel novel without treating it as proof.

Developmental Change Will Keep Creating New Uncertainty

A newborn lies where you place them.

A crawling baby does not.

A toddler climbs.

A child talks, separates, attends childcare, and develops preferences you cannot control.

The content of parental fear will change because the real parenting task changes.

Recovery therefore cannot depend on mastering one static list of triggers.

It depends on a portable process:

Find the real rule.

Notice the OCD addition.

Reduce the compulsion.

Respond to actual changes.

Ask for clinical help when the mental state or risk changes.

That process can grow with the child.

When You Are Ready to Use the Book Less

One sign of progress may be that you need this book less often.

Keep the relapse card.

Keep the appointment and emergency information.

Then let the rest sit on a shelf.

A treatment book should not become an object you must consult before every care task.

The point was always to return authority to real information, clinical care, and your chosen behavior, not to create another source of permission.

Build a Transfer Question

When a new theme appears, ask one question:

"What skill from the old theme transfers here?"

If you learned to stop reassurance after accidental-harm thoughts, the same response may fit contamination doubt.

If you learned to disclose violent obsessions accurately, you can use the same honesty with a sexual-harm theme.

If you learned to define ordinary safety around stairs, you can use the same process around driving.

Transfer keeps you from rebuilding treatment from zero.

Keep Clinical Review in the Loop

Theme transfer is a self-help principle, not a reason to skip professional review.

Tell your clinician when symptoms change substantially.

A new obsession may be handled with the same ERP model.

A new depressive episode, psychotic symptom, medical problem, substance issue, or actual change in intent may need a different plan.

You are allowed to use familiar skills while still asking whether the clinical picture changed.

The Long View

A year from now, the baby will be different.

So will the practical risks.

So may your sleep, work, relationship, and body.

A useful recovery model must tolerate change.

The stable piece is not the list of triggers.

It is the process of responding proportionately to reality while giving compulsive certainty less control.

That is the skill worth carrying forward.

Do Not Forecast Every Possible Theme

Once you learn that OCD can change subjects, you may begin trying to predict what it will choose next.

That prediction project is another form of monitoring.

You do not need to pre-expose yourself to every taboo theme.

You need a process that can be applied when a real problem appears.

If a new obsession develops, describe it.

Check whether the mechanism is familiar.

Tell the clinician when appropriate.

Use the existing skills.

Leave hypothetical future themes in the future.

Ending Treatment Without Demanding Certainty

At some point, formal treatment may become less frequent or end.

OCD can make discharge frightening.

"What if I relapse the week after?"

A good ending plan includes early signs, booster options, medication follow-up when relevant, and urgent-care instructions.

It cannot guarantee that symptoms never return.

The final exposure may be trusting a reasonable maintenance plan without keeping therapy active solely as a reassurance source.

Ending one phase of care does not remove the option to return when clinically needed.

Principles to Remember

OCD themes can change. New content may feel more significant simply because it is new.

Look for the mechanism: obsession, distress, compulsion, short relief, repeat.

Do not use pattern recognition to dismiss genuine clinical changes. New intent, psychosis, mania, severe depression, or safety impairment needs assessment.

Track relapse through behavior more than thought count.

Use early signs, early responses, booster treatment, and a clear urgent-care threshold.

Recovery is not a silent mind. It is a life in which intrusive thoughts have less power to organize your choices.

Conclusion: Parent Without Proving

The first thought in this book arrived during ordinary care.

That is where the book ends too.

A baby needs a feed, a diaper, a safe place to sleep, a ride to an appointment, a clean shirt, a few minutes of play, or another ordinary act. The mind may be quiet. It may not.

Your work is not to earn permission to care by proving what every thought means.

Harm OCD turns parenting into an investigation. It asks you to examine images, feelings, memories, anger, tenderness, bodily sensations, facial expressions, and imagined futures. It promises that one more check will settle the question.

The check rarely settles it for long.

Recovery asks for a different exchange.

You give up some certainty.

You get behavior back.

The Distinction That Matters

An intrusive obsession is not clinically identical to intent or psychosis.

That statement has carried much of the book.

It is also not a slogan to use instead of assessment.

When harm thoughts appear, clinicians need to understand how the thought is experienced, whether it is wanted, whether there is intent or planning, whether reality testing is intact, whether hallucinations or delusions are present, what mood and sleep are doing, how the person functions, and what compulsions follow.

If actual intent, a plan, psychotic symptoms, severe confusion or mania, or inability to maintain safety appears, urgent assessment is the right response.

If the pattern is assessed as OCD, treatment does not require you to prove innocence to your own mind every hour.

It asks you to change the loop.

The Loop You Now Know

You can see the sequence.

An intrusive thought.

A spike of distress or uncertainty.

A compulsion.

Relief.

A stronger rule next time.

The compulsion may be easy to spot.

Repeated checking.

Avoidance.

Washing.

Reassurance.

Or it may happen invisibly.

Review.

Testing feelings.

Reconstructing memory.

Confessing details.

Comparing yourself with strangers.

Trying to determine whether the thought felt unwanted in exactly the right way.

Once you can see the function, you have a place to intervene.

The SAFE Return in Real Life

Spot the obsession.

Allow uncertainty.

Forego the compulsion.

Engage with real care.

The method is intentionally modest.

It does not claim to cure OCD.

It does not replace ERP.

It does not classify an emergency.

It is a response direction.

When you are holding your baby and an image appears, it tells you where to place the next choice.

When you are tempted to ask your partner for the sixth reassurance answer, it gives you another move.

When you are writing a disclosure note, it helps you stop polishing the sentence until it sounds harmless.

When a new theme appears, it reminds you to look at the mechanism.

Ordinary Safety Is Still Safety

Response prevention does not ask you to become casual about a baby's needs.

Follow medical guidance.

Use safety equipment correctly.

Rest when exhaustion makes a task unsafe.

Ask for practical help.

Take a sick baby for care.

Tell a prescriber about medication questions.

Use emergency services when the mental state changes in a dangerous way.

The work is to stop adding a second layer whose purpose is not safety but certainty.

That layer can be enormous.

Removing it can make parenting feel unfamiliar at first.

You may finish a task while still anxious.

You may close a browser while the question remains.

You may leave an appointment without a guarantee about every future thought.

That is not an unfinished exposure.

That is the practice.

Disclosure Is Part of Recovery

Many readers began this book with a secret.

If that is still true, decide what your next responsible disclosure is.

Perhaps it is a GP.

An OB-GYN.

A midwife.

A health visitor.

A psychiatrist.

A therapist.

A perinatal mental health team.

A partner who needs to know you are struggling.

Use the accurate sentence.

"I have repeated unwanted thoughts or images about harming my baby, and I am frightened by them. I want an assessment for OCD and any other condition that could explain them."

Then describe intent or lack of intent, psychotic symptoms or their absence, compulsions, function, mood, sleep, and any actual safety concern.

You do not have to predict what the professional will think.

You have to give them enough truth to assess.

The Parent You Are While Recovering

OCD may have convinced you that good parenting is a feeling.

It is not only a feeling.

It is also a series of actions taken under imperfect conditions.

You can ask for help.

You can take medication if you and your clinician decide it is appropriate.

You can practice ERP while anxious.

You can feel irritated and still put the baby down safely.

You can dislike the newborn stage and still provide care.

You can have an intrusive thought and decide not to organize the day around it.

Recovery does not require a perfect internal atmosphere.

If the Thought Comes Back Tomorrow

It may.

Try not to turn recurrence into a referendum.

A thought appeared.

What is the next compulsive invitation?

Can you decline one part of it?

What is the real task?

Do that.

If symptoms are worsening, contact treatment.

If the mental state has changed in a way that affects safety or reality testing, seek appropriate assessment.

If the thought is the old obsession wearing a new shirt, use the same treatment direction.

The Final Action

Choose one ordinary parenting action you have postponed because you wanted to feel certain first.

Do not choose something unsafe.

Do not choose the hardest exposure merely because it sounds impressive.

Choose something proportionate.

A feed.

A diaper change.

A stroller walk.

A phone call to a clinician.

Ten minutes alone with the baby if your treatment plan supports it.

A nap while another safe adult takes over.

Do the action without first solving the thought.

That is the book in practice.
The mind can speak.
Real care can continue.

Resource 1: The First Seven Days After You Recognize the Pattern

Recognition can create a burst of urgency.

You discover the phrase *postpartum OCD* or *harm OCD*. The description fits. You want to read everything, fix everything, confess everything, and know immediately whether you are safe.

That burst can become another OCD project.

This seven-day plan is designed to slow the project down without delaying care. It assumes you are not in an acute emergency. If you have intent or a plan to harm yourself or your baby, psychotic symptoms, severe confusion or mania, or cannot maintain safety, seek urgent professional assessment rather than following a self-help week.

The plan is not treatment. It is a bridge from private fear to appropriate care.

Day One: Describe, Do Not Diagnose

Write a neutral description of the current pattern.

Use four short paragraphs.

First, describe the intrusive experience.

"I have unwanted images of intentionally harming my baby."

Second, describe your relationship to it.

"I do not want the images, but I am frightened by what they could mean."

Third, describe what you do afterward.

"I ask for reassurance, avoid the kitchen, and review whether I felt angry."

Fourth, describe impact.

"This takes about two hours a day and I avoid caring for the baby alone."

Do not add a final paragraph proving why you are a good person.

Do not decide that the description confirms OCD.

Its purpose is to give a clinician useful information.

If you already have a clinician, send or bring the summary according to the clinic's normal procedure.

Day Two: Identify the Urgent-Care Threshold

Make the emergency note from Chapter 3.

Write the symptoms that should move you out of self-help and into urgent assessment: actual intent or a plan to harm, hallucinations, fixed beliefs others say are not true, severe confusion, marked mania or rapid behavioral change, inability to maintain safety, or another urgent sign your clinician identifies.

Add your local route.

Emergency department.

Local emergency number.

Crisis service.

Perinatal urgent service if your region has one.

Do not use the list for hourly checking.

You are creating a plan once so the decision route is available if symptoms change.

Day Three: Make One Treatment Contact

Contact one appropriate clinician or service.

A primary-care doctor, OB-GYN, midwife, health visitor, psychiatrist, therapist, or perinatal mental health service can be an entry point depending on your health system.

Use a direct sentence.

"I am pregnant/postpartum and having repeated unwanted harm thoughts about my baby. I am responding with checking, avoidance, and reassurance. I want an assessment for OCD and other perinatal mental health conditions."

If you already have a therapist who does not treat OCD, tell them you want an OCD-specific assessment or referral.

Do not wait until you have found the perfect specialist to disclose significant symptoms.

If the first service cannot help, ask where they refer perinatal OCD.

Day Four: Find One Compulsion

Choose one behavior.

Not all of them.

Perhaps you search forums.

Perhaps you ask your partner for certainty.

Perhaps you review the thought after every feed.

Perhaps you avoid one ordinary room.

Write the cycle.

Obsession.

Distress.

Compulsion.

Relief.

Repeat.

Then choose a small change.

Delay one reassurance question.

Close one search.

Stop one round of review.

Do not select a severe trigger or remove a real safety measure without appropriate clinical guidance.

The point is to see that the loop has a behavioral part.

Day Five: Define One Ordinary Safety Rule

Pick one task that OCD has complicated.

A bottle.

A car seat.

A bath.

A staircase.

A monitor.

Find the real safety rule from a reliable source or relevant professional.

Write it in one sentence.

Then write the OCD addition underneath.

"Real rule: follow the car-seat instructions and confirm the buckle once."

"OCD addition: photograph it and ask two people to inspect the photo."

Do not remove the real rule.

Discuss the addition with your therapist if available.

This exercise trains the central distinction of the book.

Day Six: Change How You Ask for Support

Tell one support person what helps.

"I may ask you for certainty when I am anxious. If it is the same OCD question, please do not keep answering it. You can remind me of the treatment plan and help with practical tasks."

Give them the emergency exception too.

"If I tell you there is new intent, a plan, psychotic symptoms, severe confusion, or I cannot stay safe, that is different. Help me get urgent care."

Support should not require the other person to guess whether every question is reassurance.

Agree on language before the next spike.

Day Seven: Review Behavior, Not Thought Count

At the end of the week, do not ask whether intrusive thoughts disappeared.

Ask:

Did I describe the pattern more accurately?

Did I identify the urgent-care threshold?

Did I contact a professional?

Did I recognize one compulsion?

Did I define one ordinary safety rule?
Did I change one reassurance exchange?
These are actions.
If the thoughts were loud all week, the actions still count.
Then choose the next clinical step.
An assessment appointment.
An ERP consultation.
A medication review.
A partner session.
A referral.
A higher level of care if recommended.
Do not turn the seven-day plan into seven days of solo treatment.
Its purpose is to get you connected and oriented.

If You Miss a Day

Continue.
There is no catch-up requirement.
Do not combine three tasks to make the schedule "correct."
The plan is deliberately resistant to perfectionism.
The next useful action is enough.

If a Day Becomes a Ritual

You may rewrite the symptom description repeatedly.

You may reread the emergency signs.

You may contact five therapists because one answer does not feel certain.

You may refine the ordinary-safety rule until it becomes another checklist.

Notice the function.
Use a stopping rule.
One symptom page.
One emergency note.
One or two treatment contacts at a time.

One safety rule.
Then return to ordinary life.

What Success Looks Like After Seven Days

Success is not a verdict that you have OCD.

Success is a movement from secrecy toward assessment.

You have language.

You know the urgent threshold.

You have identified at least one maintaining behavior.

You have made contact with care.

You have begun separating safety from certainty.

That is enough for one week.

Resource 2: The Intrusive-Thought Appointment Guide

A good appointment does not require a polished story.

It requires accurate information.

This guide helps you prepare without writing a twenty-page defense.

Use one sheet of paper or one phone note.

The Opening Statement

Start with the hardest clinically relevant fact.

"I have repeated unwanted intrusive thoughts or images about harming my baby."

Then add the pattern.

"I do not want them, and I respond by avoiding tasks, checking my reactions, and asking for reassurance."

Then ask for assessment.

"I would like you to assess whether this is OCD and whether any other perinatal mental health condition needs to be considered."

If your thoughts are not unwanted, if you have intent, or if psychotic symptoms are present, say that accurately instead.

The guide is not a script for producing an OCD diagnosis.

The Six Domains

One: The Mental Event

Describe whether it is a thought, image, feared impulse, urge, doubt, belief, or voice.

If you cannot classify it, use sensory description.

"It is a picture in my mind."

"It feels like a sentence in my own internal voice."

"I hear a voice that seems external."

"I have a fixed belief that others tell me is not true."

Do not choose the label that feels safest.

Two: Relationship to It

Do you want it?

Do you agree with it?

Are you frightened by what it could mean?

How convinced are you that the feared interpretation is true?

Does your confidence change during spikes?

This helps the clinician understand insight and ego-dystonicity without relying on a yes-or-no shortcut.

Three: Intent, Plan, and Safety

State whether you have any intention to harm.

State whether you have made a plan.

State whether you have taken steps toward acting.

State whether you believe you can keep yourself and the baby safe.

If you are unsure, say you are unsure.

This domain should never be edited to fit a preferred diagnosis.

Four: What You Do Next

List the main compulsions or safety behaviors.

Checking.

Avoidance.

Reassurance.

Rumination.

Confession.

Internet searching.

Body checking.

Mental review.

Repeated washing or cleaning.

Transferring infant care.

Describe frequency or time in rough terms.

The purpose is to show the cycle.

Five: Other Symptoms

Tell the clinician about depression, suicidal thoughts, panic, trauma symptoms, hallucinations, fixed beliefs, severe confusion, unusual energy, major sleep changes, substance use, eating problems, or medical issues.

Do not assume a symptom is irrelevant because OCD fits part of the picture.

Perinatal assessment is broader than one diagnosis.

Six: Function and Support

What tasks have changed?

Can you eat?

Can you sleep when you have the opportunity?

Can you complete ordinary infant care?

Can you leave the house?

Can you work?

Who helps you?

Is home safe?

What does your partner or family observe?

Function helps determine severity and level of care.

The Timeline

Write approximate dates.

Before pregnancy: relevant mental health history.

Pregnancy: first symptoms or major changes.

Birth: important medical or psychiatric events.

Postpartum: when symptoms worsened or changed.

Current: what is happening now.

Approximate dates are enough.

Do not spend an hour trying to remember whether a thought first appeared on a Tuesday or Wednesday unless the date matters medically.

Medication List

Bring all current prescription medicines.

Include over-the-counter medicines and supplements if your clinician asks for them.

Include dose and frequency.

Note recent changes.

If you stopped a psychiatric medication around pregnancy, tell the clinician when and why.

Medication history can affect both differential diagnosis and treatment planning.

Treatment History

List previous therapy.

Was it general counseling?

CBT?

ERP?

Trauma-focused treatment?

A perinatal program?

What helped?

What became reassurance?

What did you stop because of side effects, access, cost, or fit?

A clinician does not need a favorable treatment history.

They need an accurate one.

Questions to Ask

"What diagnoses are you considering?"

"How are you distinguishing intrusive obsessions from intent or psychosis?"

"Do you treat OCD with ERP, or can you refer me?"

"What symptoms should make me seek urgent help?"

"What are the confidentiality and safeguarding rules here?"

"If medication is being considered, who can review pregnancy or breastfeeding factors?"

"What role should my partner or support person have?"

"When will we review whether the plan is working?"

Choose the questions that matter.

You do not need to ask all eight in one rushed visit.

If Safeguarding Is Your Main Fear

Say so.

"I have been afraid to disclose because I am worried about child-protection consequences. Can you explain your safeguarding duties and how you assess risk when harm thoughts may be obsessional?"

The clinician may not be able to promise a particular outcome.

They should be able to explain their role and the next steps as far as the situation allows.

If they need to consult a safeguarding team, ask what that process usually involves.

Do not hide material that changes actual risk in an attempt to avoid the process.

If You Freeze

Hand over the note.

A written disclosure is still a disclosure.

You can say:

"I find this very hard to say aloud. Please read this first, then ask me what you need."

If the note includes an urgent safety concern, tell the receptionist or clinician rather than waiting until the end of the appointment.

If You Minimize

Some parents smile while describing severe symptoms.

Some use humor.

Some say, "It is not that bad" after explaining that they have not been alone with the baby for a month.

Clinicians should assess behavior and function, not only tone.

Help them by using concrete examples.

"I have stopped all diaper changes."

"I spend three hours a day reviewing."

"I have not slept despite having the opportunity."

"I am hearing a voice."

"I have a plan to harm myself."

Concrete information reduces reliance on how distressed you appear.

If You Overexplain

OCD may push you to provide every detail.

Set a boundary.

Give enough content to identify the theme.

Answer follow-up questions.

Then move to the pattern and risk domains.

You do not need to prove your innocence by telling the clinician every thought you have ever had.

If you notice a compulsion to add one more detail after the visit, ask whether the detail changes assessment or risk.

If it does, share it.

If it does not, bring the urge to therapy.

After the Appointment

Write the plan in plain language.

Diagnosis or working formulation.

Treatment referral.

Medication action if any.

Safety plan.

Urgent signs.

Follow-up date.

Who to call with questions.

Then stop reviewing the clinician's facial expressions.

If you genuinely do not understand a plan, ask for clarification once.

If the question is "Did the clinician secretly think I was dangerous despite everything she said?", that may be the OCD question returning.

The Appointment Guide in One Paragraph

I am having ______ (type of mental event) about ______ (theme). It is ______ (wanted, unwanted, or unclear). I ______ (do, do not, or am unsure whether I) have intent or a plan. I ______ (do or do not) have hallucinations, fixed beliefs, severe confusion, or marked mood and energy changes. After the thought I ______ (main compulsions). This takes ______ (rough time) and affects ______ (main functions). My relevant history is ______ (brief history). I want an assessment and a treatment plan, including what should make me seek urgent help.

That paragraph is enough to begin.

Resource 3: A Partner Guide for the Hard Hour

This resource is written for the person standing beside the parent with OCD.

Your job is not to become a risk assessor.

Your job is not to say the perfect thing.

Your job is to know the treatment plan, recognize when the situation has genuinely changed, reduce reassurance rituals when that is part of treatment, and provide practical human support.

If you are worried that the parent has intent to harm, a plan, psychotic symptoms, severe confusion or mania, or cannot maintain safety, seek professional help. Do not rely on a self-help script.

First, Believe the Distress

An intrusive thought can sound terrible.

The person may be ashamed to say it.

You can take the distress seriously without deciding what the thought means.

Try:

"Thank you for telling me."

"I can hear that this is frightening."

"Let's use the assessment or treatment plan."

Do not demand every graphic detail.

Do not tell the person to stop thinking it.

Do not make a diagnosis from one sentence.

Second, Know the Formulation

If the person has been assessed and consents to your involvement, learn the basic formulation.

What are the main obsessions?

What are the main compulsions?

What reassurance do you usually provide?

What tasks are you doing only because of OCD avoidance?

What are the urgent signs?

Who is the clinician?

What should happen if symptoms worsen?

A partner session with the therapist can be useful when available.

The purpose is alignment.

Third, Separate Practical Help From Reassurance

A parent says, "Can you take the baby?"

Ask what is needed.

If the person has not slept and needs rest, taking the baby is practical help.

If the person is working through a graded exposure to being alone and asks you to take over solely because anxiety rose, the treatment plan may say to support them differently.

Do not guess.

Use the plan.

Practical help can be generous.

Meals.

Laundry.

Appointments.

Protected rest.

Older-child care.

Transport.

Insurance calls.

Medication pickup.

Treatment does not require withholding normal support.

Fourth, Use One Reassurance Boundary

Pick a repeated question.

"Do you think I would hurt the baby?"

Agree that you will not answer it repeatedly after clinical assessment has addressed the concern and no new information is present.

Use a short response.

"I know you want certainty. I am not going to answer that OCD question again. I can stay with you while you follow the plan."

Then stop explaining.

If you supply ten reasons, those reasons may become ten items the person checks tomorrow.

Fifth, Make Room for New Information

A reassurance boundary must not silence safety disclosure.

If the parent says:

"I have a plan."

"I want to act."

"I hear a voice telling me to do something."

"I believe something about the baby that everyone says is untrue."

"I have barely slept and I feel intensely energized and unlike myself."

"I cannot keep the baby safe."

Treat that as new clinical information.

Use the urgent plan.

Do not answer, "That is just your OCD" unless a qualified clinician has assessed the current change and told you what to do.

Sixth, Watch Accommodation Without Becoming the Police

You may notice rituals the person does not.

Repeated checks.

Transferred care.

Questions disguised as conversation.

Online searches.

Avoided rooms.

You do not need to point out every event.

Choose the targets agreed in treatment.

If you police all behavior, the relationship becomes another monitoring system.

You can say:

"I think this might be the pattern we agreed to watch. Do you want to use the plan?"

Then let the person do the skill.

Seventh, Protect Your Own Capacity

Supporting a person with severe OCD can be tiring.

You are also adjusting to a baby.

You may have work, other children, financial pressure, and your own mental health.

Ask for support.

Tell the clinician if accommodation is consuming the household.

Share tasks with other safe adults when possible.

Take your own rest.

If you feel resentment, discuss the practical problem in daylight rather than exploding during a reassurance loop.

Your exhaustion is relevant to the family plan.

Eighth, Do Not Make Yourself the Sole Gatekeeper

You should not be the only person deciding whether symptoms are urgent.

Keep professional contacts.

Know the local emergency route.

Encourage the parent to attend appointments.

If you observe a marked change that the parent cannot recognize, contact appropriate services according to the care plan.

The family needs a clinical network, not a single exhausted witness.

Ninth, Keep Ordinary Life Present

OCD can become the household's only subject.

Talk about something else.

Watch a show.

Take a walk.

Discuss the grocery list.

Send a photo to a grandparent.

Plan a meal.

Laugh when something is funny.

Ordinary life is not avoidance when the treatment plan is already in place. It is the life treatment is trying to return.

Tenth, Repair When You Get It Wrong

You will reassure sometimes.

You may become impatient.

You may say a clumsy thing after hearing a frightening thought.

Repair.

"I gave reassurance because I was scared. Next time I want to use the plan."

"I was harsh. I am sorry."

"I need a break, and I still care."

A partner guide should not create another perfection standard.

Consistency matters more than flawless technique.

Resource 4: Questions Worth Asking, Questions OCD Wants Answered Forever

Not every question should be resisted.

The problem is not curiosity.

The problem is a question with no workable stopping rule that is asked to produce certainty.

This resource helps you separate the two.

Worth Asking: "What Treatment Do You Recommend?"

This is a decision question.

A clinician can answer based on assessment.

You may need ERP.

Medication.

A combination.

A referral.

A higher level of care.

A plan for depression or trauma too.

The answer may change with symptoms.

That is appropriate.

OCD Forever Question: "Can You Promise This Thought Will Never Mean Anything?"

No clinician can give a permanent guarantee about every future internal event.

Repeatedly asking invites repeated reassurance.

A better question is:

"How should I respond when I feel the need for certainty about the thought?"

That can produce a treatment plan.

Worth Asking: "What Symptoms Are an Emergency?"

This produces an action threshold.

Write the answer.

Use it when circumstances change.

Do not reread it every hour.

OCD Forever Question: "Do I Have Exactly Enough Insight to Be Safe?"

Insight is clinically relevant.

Turning it into a minute-by-minute measurement is not useful.

Tell the clinician when your ability to question beliefs changes.

Do not grade yourself all day.

Worth Asking: "What Is the Ordinary Safety Rule?"

Ask once when you genuinely do not know.

How should this medication be stored?

When should I call about a fever?

How should this equipment be used?

What does the pediatric guideline say?

Then follow the answer.

OCD Forever Question: "What If the Ordinary Rule Misses a One-in-a-Million Event?"

No ordinary rule removes all theoretical risk.

If no new evidence exists, this is usually the uncertainty layer.

Discuss the pattern in ERP.

Worth Asking: "How Do Your Confidentiality and Safeguarding Rules Work?"

This is a real policy question.

Professionals can explain their duties and limits.

OCD Forever Question: "Can You Guarantee Nobody Will Ever Misunderstand Me?"

No.

You can communicate accurately.

You can ask for specialist input.

You can seek a second opinion where available.

You cannot control every interpretation.

Worth Asking: "Could This Medication Help My OCD, and What Are the Perinatal Risks?"

A prescriber can discuss the evidence.

OCD Forever Question: "Can You Prove There Is Zero Risk to the Baby From Every Treatment Choice?"

Medicine rarely works in zero-risk terms.

Ask for known benefits, risks, alternatives, and uncertainty.

Then make the decision with the clinician.

Worth Asking: "What Compulsion Should I Target First?"

An ERP therapist can help choose a behavior.

OCD Forever Question: "Did I Perform ERP Perfectly?"

Treatment is not a purity test.

Ask whether the practice targeted the right mechanism and how to adjust next time.

Then move on.

Worth Asking: "What Has Actually Changed?"

This may be the most useful relapse question.

New intent?

New psychotic symptoms?

New depression?

New medical issue?

New functional loss?

More rituals?

A new theme with the same old mechanism?

Describe the change.

OCD Forever Question: "Why This Exact Thought?"

Sometimes there is a useful trigger.

Sometimes there is not.

If the question has no practical consequence and you have already reviewed it repeatedly, leave it.

Your life does not need a complete origin story for every mental event.

A Stopping Rule for Questions

Before you ask, decide what kind of answer could end the task.

If no possible answer would be enough, the question may be asking for certainty rather than information.

If a specific professional can provide information that changes a decision, ask.

If you already have the information and the only missing piece is a feeling of certainty, use response prevention.

This is not a perfect distinction.

It is a workable one.

Resource 5: A Field Guide to Hidden Compulsions

Visible compulsions get attention because another person can see them.

Mental compulsions can occupy an entire day while the outside of life appears unchanged.

This field guide names common hidden moves and gives each one a different stopping response. It is not a diagnostic checklist. A behavior becomes clinically relevant through its function, repetition, distress, and impact, and a qualified clinician should assess your individual pattern.

Use the guide to notice possibilities, not to count how many forms of OCD you have.

The Replay

The replay is a mental video review.

You return to the moment when the thought appeared.

Where were your hands?

What expression was on your face?

Did the image begin before or after you felt angry?

Did you move closer or farther away?

The replay promises a factual answer.

After several rounds, memory usually feels less trustworthy rather than more.

Different move: State the one fact that matters for present care, if there is one. If there was no new safety event to report, decline another viewing.

"I have already reviewed this. I am not watching it again."

Then use your attention on a current task.

The Feeling Check

The feeling check asks whether you reacted correctly.

Were you disgusted enough?

Scared enough?

Loving enough?

Relieved too quickly?

Too calm?

Too numb?

A feeling can become suspicious in every direction.

If you are very distressed, OCD says the thought must be serious.

If you are calm, OCD says the lack of distress proves you wanted it.

There is no passing score.

Different move: Stop using emotion as a lie detector. If persistent numbness, depression, or major mood change needs clinical assessment, tell a clinician. Otherwise let the feeling be ungraded.

The Character File

The character file collects evidence from your past.

Kind acts go in one column.

Irritated moments go in another.

You search childhood memories for cruelty.

You remember arguments.

You compare what you have done with what a "good mother" would do.

No file can prove a future in absolute terms.

The more material you collect, the more ambiguous material appears.

Different move: Close the moral archive. Let current behavior and professional assessment handle current responsibilities.

The "What Would a Dangerous Person Do?" Test

You imagine a dangerous person.

Would they feel guilty?

Would they search for reassurance?

Would they read a book like this?

Would they tell a therapist?

Then you compare yourself.

Even if the comparison reassures you, the next obsession can change the imagined profile.

Different move: Do not diagnose safety by stereotype. Describe your actual symptoms, intent or lack of intent, behavior, reality testing, and function to a clinician.

The Body Scan

You inspect your hands, heart rate, stomach, genitals, muscle tension, or another bodily signal.

The question is not medical.

It is moral.

"What did that sensation mean?"

Attention magnifies sensation.

Ambiguous sensation creates more checking.

Different move: If there is a medical symptom, address it medically. If the scan is being used to answer the obsession, stop the scan and return to the task.

The Rehearsed Reassurance

You know exactly what your partner will say.

You ask anyway.

The wording may be slightly disguised.

"You still trust me with her, right?"

"You did not notice anything strange, did you?"

"I am probably overthinking this, yes?"

The answer works briefly because it comes from someone else.

Different move: Ask for company or practical help without asking for a verdict.

"Can you sit with me for five minutes while I let this question remain unanswered?"

The Professional Recheck

You have already asked the clinician.

Then you change one word.

"What if the image lasted ten seconds instead of five?"

"What if I felt angry earlier?"

"What if I was less distressed this time?"

Some changes are clinically relevant. Many are new versions of the same certainty question.

Different move: Agree with the clinician on what changes should trigger reassessment. Bring genuinely new risk information. Handle the rest as OCD.

The Confession Urge

You feel dishonest until you report every thought.

You tell your partner.

Relief.

Then remember a detail.

Tell it too.

Relief.

Then worry that the order was wrong.

Confess again.

Different move: Share information that is needed for assessment, safety, or normal relationship communication. Do not use another person's reaction as absolution.

The Internet Match

You search for someone whose thought was exactly like yours.

Not merely violent.

Not merely postpartum.

The same setting.

The same sensation.

The same emotional response.

The closer the match, the more relief.

Then one detail differs.

Different move: Use the internet for finding care and reputable education. Do not use strangers as diagnostic twins.

The Language Test

You become preoccupied with whether the thought was an "urge," an "impulse," an "image," or an "intention."

Clinical language matters.

Compulsive language analysis uses labels to manufacture certainty.

You may spend an hour deciding whether a sensation qualified as a true urge.

Different move: Describe the experience to the clinician in ordinary words. "It felt like a sudden pull that I did not want, and I became afraid of it." Let the clinician ask follow-up questions.

The Timing Test

"Did the anger happen first?"

"Did I think the thought before I looked at the baby?"

"Was I already anxious?"

You try to reconstruct a timeline down to seconds.

The assumption is that the sequence will prove motive.

Different move: Give a rough sequence if it matters clinically. Refuse microscopic reconstruction for certainty.

The Frequency Test

You count how many times the thought appears.

Five seems acceptable.

Twenty feels dangerous.

Then you notice you are monitoring constantly.

Counting makes the thought easier to detect.

Different move: Track functional impact and compulsions if your clinician wants data. Do not use thought count as a safety score.

The Disgust Test

Sexual-harm obsessions can produce repeated attempts to measure disgust.

"If I am disgusted, that proves something."

Then disgust fades through repetition or exhaustion.

Panic follows.

Different move: Do not turn disgust into a diagnostic instrument. Tell the clinician the content and your relationship to it. Treatment targets the checking, not a required level of revulsion.

The Love Test

You look at the baby and ask whether love appears.

If it does, relief.

If it does not, fear.

Soon every interaction is a scan.

Different move: Choose one care action and complete it without measuring the emotional result.

The Avoidance Justification

You stop a task.

Then build a reasonable-sounding explanation.

"My partner is better at baths."

"I never liked cooking anyway."

"I am too busy to take the stairs."

Sometimes those statements are true.

Ask whether the behavior changed after an obsession and whether the rule exists mainly to prevent uncertainty.

Different move: Bring the pattern to treatment and reclaim the task gradually if it is safe and appropriate.

The Overpreparation Ritual

You prepare for an appointment by writing five pages.

Then ten.

You create categories.

Cross-reference symptoms.

Rewrite sentences so they cannot be misunderstood.

Preparation becomes an attempt to control the assessor.

Different move: Use the one-page appointment guide. One revision for clarity. Stop.

The Research Stack

You save papers, screenshots, podcast episodes, and forum threads.

The stack feels responsible.

You rarely use it to make a decision.

You use it to keep the possibility of more certainty available.

Different move: Keep a small set of trusted sources. New research should answer a real decision question, not an identity question.

The Thought Replacement

An image appears.

You force in a happy image.

A violent word appears.

You repeat a loving phrase.

The replacement gives relief and becomes mandatory.

Different move: Let the unwanted thought exist without adding the corrective thought on purpose. Return to behavior.

The Prayer or Moral Neutralization

Prayer can be a normal religious practice.

It can also become compulsive when repeated according to rigid rules solely to cancel a thought or prevent harm.

The same is true of moral self-statements.

Different move: If faith matters to you, discuss the pattern with an OCD-informed clinician and, if helpful, a trusted faith leader who understands scrupulosity. Keep ordinary spiritual practice separate from emergency neutralization.

The "Just Checking the Plan" Ritual

You read the SAFE Return card.

Again.

Again.

Again.

Now the treatment tool is functioning as reassurance.

Different move: Use the card once to orient. Then put it away and do the action.

The Post-Exposure Review

You complete an ERP task.

Then spend thirty minutes asking whether you did it correctly.

Did you secretly reassure yourself?

Did you avoid one small part?

Was your anxiety high enough?

Treatment becomes a performance audit.

Different move: Record one behavioral fact if your therapist wants it. "Completed planned feed without asking partner for reassurance." Save detailed review for the scheduled session.

The Future Simulation

You imagine every possible future situation.

"What if I am angry and alone?"

"What if I have not slept?"

"What if the baby is a toddler and can reach things?"

"What if the thought changes?"

Planning is useful up to a point.

Simulation becomes compulsive when it tries to pre-solve every future uncertainty.

Different move: Create plans for likely or high-impact situations with real stopping points. Leave hypothetical scenarios for when they become relevant.

The Retrospective Diagnosis

You search your childhood for signs you were "always this way."

You reinterpret every odd thought.

You create a lifetime OCD theory.

A clinician may ask about history, and history can matter.

The compulsion is the demand for a perfect retrospective diagnosis.

Different move: Give relevant history in broad strokes. Let uncertainty remain where memory is incomplete.

The Comparison Compulsion

You compare your symptoms with another parent.

"She had images, but mine are words."

"She was scared immediately, but I was numb."

"Her baby was three months old, but mine is six weeks."

Differences become reasons the diagnosis may not apply.

Different move: Use clinical criteria and assessment, not stranger matching.

The Risk-Percentage Game

You want a number.

"How likely am I to act?"

No general book can calculate individual risk.

A clinician may discuss risk qualitatively based on the whole presentation.

OCD may still want 0.000 percent.

Different move: Ask what level of care is appropriate now and what changes require reassessment. Use an action threshold rather than a fantasy of numerical certainty.

The "One Last Time" Ritual

This is the oldest trick.

One last search.

One last question.

One last review.

One last check.

The phrase appears because part of you already knows the behavior has stopped being useful.

Different move: Treat "one last time" as a cue to stop now.

How to Use This Field Guide

Choose one hidden compulsion that appears often.

Do not try to eliminate all twenty-five.

Name the trigger.

Name the operation.

Name the short-term relief.

Choose one small response-prevention action.

Practice it for several days or as agreed with your therapist.
When another compulsion becomes obvious, add it later.
The purpose is not mastery of a list.
It is learning to recognize the job a behavior is doing.

Resource 6: A Four-Week Practice Companion

This resource is for a reader who has already sought or is seeking professional assessment and wants a simple way to organize the ideas in the book.

It is not a substitute for treatment.

If you have not been assessed and symptoms are significant, use the first week to make that contact.

If you have urgent symptoms, use urgent care.

The four weeks focus on behavior rather than thought elimination.

Week One: See the Loop

The first week has one aim: make one obsession-compulsion cycle visible.

Do not build a complete symptom inventory.

Choose the pattern that costs the most time or interferes most with ordinary care.

Perhaps it is reassurance after diapering.

Perhaps it is checking the baby's breathing.

Perhaps it is avoiding the kitchen.

Perhaps it is rumination after a violent image.

Write the loop in four lines.

Obsession.

Distress.

Compulsion.

Relief.

For seven days, notice when that loop appears.

You do not need to count every episode.

At the end of each day, record one example.

This creates enough information to discuss with a therapist without turning monitoring into a full-time job.

Week One Clinical Task

If you do not already have care, contact an appropriate professional.

Use the six-sentence disclosure.

Ask for assessment.

If you already have care, tell the clinician which loop you selected.

Week One Family Task

Tell one support person what you are working on.

Not the entire book.

One loop.

"After diapering I ask you to tell me I am safe. I want to reduce that reassurance."

Agree on one response.

Week One Safety Task

Write the urgent-care threshold once.

Do not use it for repeated checking.

End of Week One

Ask:

What compulsion gives the fastest relief?

What does the relief cost later?

What ordinary activity has become smaller?

Choose one response-prevention target for Week Two.

Week Two: Reduce One Compulsion

Do not aim at the hardest trigger.

Choose a repetition you can alter.

If you ask five reassurance questions, reduce to four or delay the first.

If you search for thirty minutes, close the browser after fifteen or skip one search period.

If you replay the thought ten times, stop when you notice the second loop.

If you avoid one low-risk ordinary task that your clinician agrees is appropriate, re-enter part of it.

The target should be specific enough to know whether you did it.

"Ruminate less" is vague.

"After the morning feed, I will not replay the image a second time" is behavioral.

Week Two: Expect the Urge

Removing a compulsion may increase discomfort.

That does not mean the compulsion was necessary.

The urge is part of what you are practicing.

Use the SAFE Return.

Spot.

Allow.

Forego.

Engage.

Then continue the day.

Week Two: No Compensation

Watch for a substitute ritual.

You stop asking your partner and start searching.

You stop searching and begin self-reassurance.

You stop checking the baby's breathing and start staring at the monitor.

The form changes.

The job stays the same.

If you find a substitute, do not declare the week ruined.

Bring it into the formulation.

Week Two Clinical Task

Tell the therapist what happened when you reduced the compulsion.

Use behavior, not self-judgment.

"I delayed reassurance by five minutes on four days. Twice I replaced it with online searching."

That is useful treatment information.

End of Week Two

Ask:

Did I reduce the chosen behavior at all?

What substitute appeared?

What real support did I need?

What made practice easier to repeat?

Then decide whether to keep the same target or move one step.

Week Three: Reclaim an Ordinary Task

OCD often takes a normal parenting activity and makes it conditional.

This week selects one task to reclaim.

The task might be:

A routine diaper change.

A stroller walk.

A normal kitchen activity.

Holding the baby in a place you have avoided.

Being alone for a short, planned period if the clinical assessment supports it.

Using stairs under ordinary safe conditions.

Choose the task with your clinician when risk feels confusing.

Define Ordinary Safety

Write the real rule first.

What medical, pediatric, equipment, or practical guidance applies?

If you do not know, ask the relevant professional.

Then write the OCD addition.

The exposure targets the addition.

Build Three Steps

Easier.

Middle.

Harder.

Make "harder" more ordinary, not more dangerous.

Example:

Easier: diaper change while partner is in the next room, no body checking.

Middle: diaper change with partner elsewhere in the house, no reassurance afterward.

Harder: ordinary diaper change while alone during an agreed period, no checking or confession.

Your hierarchy will differ.

Practice Repetition, Not Perfection

Schedule several repetitions.

Do not wait until you feel ready.

Do not add extra repetitions to test yourself.

If one practice goes poorly, resume at the next scheduled opportunity.

Week Three Clinical Task

Review whether the exposure is targeting avoidance and compulsions rather than real safety.

Ask whether mental rituals are slipping through.

Week Three Family Task

Reduce one accommodation related to the task.

The partner may stop supervising.

Or stop performing the final check.

Or stay present but refuse reassurance.

Change one piece at a time.

End of Week Three

Ask:

What part of the task is more available to me?

Which compulsion remains strongest?

Did I turn the exposure into a test?

What is the next ordinary step?

Week Four: Build the Maintenance Plan

The fourth week is not graduation.

It is a shift from one practice target to a maintenance structure.

Choose three early signs of worsening.

Behavioral signs are best.

More searching.

More reassurance.

More avoidance.

Hiding new themes.

Skipping treatment.

Longer rumination.

Write three responses.

Contact the therapist.

Return to the last exposure step.

Restore the partner boundary.

Book a medication review.

Increase practical support.

Use a booster session.

Add two contact points.

One clinical.

One personal.

Add the urgent-care threshold.

Now the plan fits on one page.

Week Four: Practice a Theme Shift

You do not need to invent graphic thoughts.

Take a benign hypothetical theme.

"What if my OCD switches from accidental harm to contamination?"

Write how the mechanism might remain the same.

Obsession.

Uncertainty.

Compulsion.

Relief.

Then write how the SAFE Return transfers.

The exercise teaches you not to treat new subject matter as proof that old skills vanished.

Week Four: Redefine Progress

Write three measures that do not depend on thought disappearance.

"I complete diaper changes without reassurance."

"I spend less time reviewing."

"I can tell my therapist a new theme without hiding it."

"I follow the ordinary safety rule once."

"I return to work without monitoring childcare updates all day."

"I ask for practical help instead of moral certainty."

Pick three.

These are your markers.

What If Four Weeks Pass and You Are Worse?

Tell the clinician.

Possible reasons include an inaccurate formulation, untreated depression or another condition, a hierarchy that is poorly designed, inadequate treatment intensity, medication issues, severe sleep disruption, medical problems, or a need for a higher level of care.

Do not conclude that you failed.

A worsening course is clinical information.

If symptoms become urgent, use urgent care.

What If You Are Better?

Keep the plan.

Do not celebrate by testing whether you are "cured."

Continue ordinary life.

Let an intrusive thought be a thought.

Use booster support when needed.

Recovery can become boring.

That is a good direction for a disorder that has demanded so much attention.

The Four-Week Plan in One View

Week One: See one loop and connect with care.

Week Two: Reduce one compulsion.

Week Three: Reclaim one ordinary task.

Week Four: Build maintenance and relapse responses.

Then repeat the structure with another target as appropriate.

You do not need a new philosophy every month.

You need repeated practice in giving uncertainty less control over behavior.

Resource 7: A Short Guide for Clinicians and Support People Reading Along

This book is written for parents, but clinicians and support people may read it to understand the language the parent is using.

The central distinction is not "harm thought equals safe" versus "harm thought equals dangerous."

The book repeatedly directs assessment toward the full presentation.

That includes whether the mental event is an unwanted obsession, a belief, a hallucination, or another phenomenon; whether intent or planning is present; insight and reality testing; compulsions and avoidance; mood and psychotic symptoms; sleep; function; infant care; medical and substance factors; history; supports; and current safety.

The reason for this emphasis is practical.

A parent who fears disclosure may omit the content.

A professional unfamiliar with OCD may overfocus on content.

A parent with OCD may use any reassuring phrase as a ritual.

A parent with psychosis may need urgent care that an OCD formulation cannot provide.

The assessment has to stay wider than the slogan.

When the Parent Uses SAFE

SAFE means Spot the obsession, Allow uncertainty, Forego the compulsion, Engage with real care.

It is a memory aid, not a standalone treatment protocol.

A clinician can help the parent determine where ordinary safety ends and OCD safety rules begin.

The tool works best when connected to a real case formulation and ERP plan.

If the parent begins repeating SAFE until anxiety falls, the tool has become part of the ritual and should be simplified.

When a Partner Uses This Book

Partners are asked to reduce repeated certainty-giving while preserving warmth and practical support.

They are also told not to become sole risk assessors.

A partner should have clear instructions about what changes require professional contact or urgent care.

The person with OCD should not be forced to prove safety repeatedly to the partner.

The partner should not be forced to pretend that all symptoms are harmless.

A shared clinical plan makes both positions less likely.

When Safeguarding Is Discussed

The book does not promise that disclosure can never lead to safeguarding action.

It states that laws and thresholds differ and that actual decisions depend on assessed risk and local duties.

It also points to perinatal standards that tell clinicians to consider that harm-related phenomena may be intrusive obsessional thoughts.

This is deliberate.

Fear of automatic punishment can silence the patient.

False promises can undermine safety.

Accurate assessment language is the middle path.

When Medication Is Discussed

The book names SSRIs because they are established OCD medications.

It does not recommend a particular drug or dose.

Pregnancy and breastfeeding decisions are kept with an appropriate prescriber.

The parent is encouraged to ask about the specific medicine, known risks, uncertainty, untreated-illness risk, alternatives, prior response, and follow-up.

If medication research becomes compulsive, the parent is encouraged to set trusted sources and a stopping rule with the prescriber.

The Desired Reader Outcome

The desired outcome is not certainty.

It is a parent who can describe symptoms accurately, obtain appropriate assessment, identify compulsions, use ERP-informed response prevention, maintain ordinary infant safety, involve support without building a reassurance system, and recognize changes that need urgent care.

That is the standard against which the book should be used.

Resource 8: Words for Hard Moments

A frightened mind often has more language than a frightened person.

OCD can produce a hundred arguments in seconds while you cannot find one sentence to say to a partner or clinician.

The scripts here are not reassurance statements. They are communication tools. Use the shortest version that tells the truth and moves you toward care.

Do not repeat a script until anxiety disappears.

When You Need to Tell a Partner for the First Time

"I have been having unwanted intrusive thoughts about harm coming to the baby, including thoughts that scare me because they involve me. I do not want to keep hiding this. I want an assessment for OCD and other postpartum mental health problems, and I would like your help making the appointment."

If intent is present, change the wording.

"I am having thoughts of harm and I am worried that I might act. I need urgent help and I do not want to be the only person managing this."

If you are unsure, say that.

"I cannot tell whether this is an intrusive fear or something more serious. I need a professional to assess it."

The point is accuracy.

When a Partner Asks for Every Detail

"I want to tell you enough to understand what is happening, but I do not want us to turn this into repeated confession. The theme is intentional harm. The thoughts are unwanted. I am going to give the full clinically relevant pattern to the person assessing me."

If the partner needs information for immediate safety, answer it.

If the request is driven by mutual reassurance, bring the pattern to treatment.

When You Need an Appointment

"I am pregnant/postpartum and experiencing repeated unwanted intrusive thoughts about harming my baby. I have started avoiding care tasks and doing repeated checking and reassurance. I would like a mental health assessment that considers perinatal OCD and other conditions."

A receptionist may not know what perinatal OCD is.

You do not need to teach them.

Ask for the appropriate mental health appointment or referral.

When the Clinician Asks, "Do You Want to Act?"

Answer directly.

"No. I do not want to act. I am frightened that the thought might mean I could."

Or:

"Yes. I am worried because I do have an intention to act."

Or:

"I am not sure. I need you to help assess what I am experiencing."

Do not add ten minutes of evidence about why your answer should be believed.

The clinician will ask what they need.

When the Clinician Asks About Voices or Beliefs

"I do not hear a voice outside my own thoughts."

Or:

"I hear a voice that seems external."

"I know the image is in my mind."

Or:

"I believe this is literally true, even though my family says it is not."

If the distinction is confusing:

"I am having trouble telling what is real and I need urgent assessment."

Plain language is better than guessing the clinical term.

When You Are Afraid of Safeguarding

"I have been afraid to disclose this because I am worried about child-protection consequences. Can you explain your confidentiality and safeguarding duties, and how you assess risk when a parent reports possible obsessional harm thoughts?"

Do not ask for a guarantee that no report can occur.

Ask for the rules and the clinical reasoning.

When a Clinician Does Not Seem Familiar With OCD

"I want to make sure the full pattern is considered. The thoughts are unwanted, and afterward I check, avoid, seek reassurance, and review my reactions. Are you considering OCD in the differential?"

Then:

"If OCD is a possibility, can you refer me to someone who treats it with ERP?"

If the clinician has an immediate safety concern, let them explain it.

Do not use OCD language to block assessment.

When You Want Reassurance From a Partner

Instead of:

"Tell me I would never hurt the baby."

Try:

"I am having the same certainty urge. Please do not answer it. Could you stay with me while I do the next ordinary task?"

Or:

"This is a rough OCD spike. I need practical help with dinner, not an answer about what the thought means."

This lets support remain specific.

When the Partner Reassures You Automatically

"Thank you for trying to help. I think that answer is becoming part of the loop. Next time, can you remind me that we are not solving the same question again?"

No blame is needed.

The reassurance developed because both people wanted relief.

Now both people are learning another response.

When You Need a Break From the Baby

"I am overloaded and need twenty minutes off duty. I am asking for rest, not because the intrusive thought proves I am dangerous."

If you are genuinely afraid you may lose control:

"I am too overwhelmed to manage safely right now. Please take over while I get help."

The same action, handing over care, can have different reasons.

State the reason honestly.

When You Need to Put the Baby Down Safely

"I am getting overwhelmed. I am going to put the baby in the safe place we use and step away briefly."

This is practical regulation.

Do not stay in a difficult caregiving moment to prove something to OCD.

If you have intent to harm, add professional help to the action.

When a Thought Hits During Diapering

Use the smallest SAFE Return.

"Intrusive image. I am not checking what it means. Finish the ordinary care."

Then finish if it is safe and consistent with your treatment plan.

Do not repeat the sentence.

When a Thought Hits on the Stairs

"Image, not new physical evidence. Use the ordinary safety rule."

If you are dizzy, physically impaired, or dangerously fatigued, the ordinary rule may be not to use the stairs while carrying the baby.

Real conditions get real responses.

When a Sexual-Harm Obsession Appears

"Unwanted sexual-harm thought. I am not checking my body for a verdict."

If the theme is new or has never been assessed, tell the clinician.

If it has been assessed as OCD, follow the ERP plan rather than collecting reassurance.

When You Feel Numb

"I notice numbness and the urge to treat it as evidence. I will tell my clinician if the numbness is persistent or part of depression, and I will not test love right now."

Then choose one ordinary care action.

This keeps clinical symptoms visible without turning every emotional shift into an OCD trial.

When Anger and a Harm Thought Arrive Together

First ask the behavioral question.

"Can I care safely right now?"

If no, put the baby in a safe place, involve another safe adult if available, and get help.

If yes, and the pattern is obsessional:

"I was angry and a harm thought appeared. I am not reviewing the anger for proof."

Feelings can be discussed in treatment without becoming forensic evidence.

When You Want to Search Online

"What decision will this search change?"

If you need a therapist directory, search.

If you need the clinic number, search.

If you want another person to tell you the thought means nothing, do not search.

Write:

"No decision. Reassurance search."

Then close the browser.

When You Want to Message the Clinician Again

Ask:

"Is there new clinical information?"

New intent.

New psychotic symptoms.

New medication reaction.

New severe depression.

A major functional change.

A question the clinician asked you to send.

Those deserve contact according to the care plan.

If the message is "Can you reassure me one more time that this is OCD?", wait and bring the reassurance pattern to treatment.

When You Are Starting ERP Practice

"My goal is not to prove safety. My goal is to do the planned ordinary action and reduce the compulsion."

That sentence protects the purpose of the exposure.

If you catch yourself testing:

"I turned the exposure into a test. I am returning to uncertainty."

No restart is required.

When ERP Felt Messy

"I completed part of the practice and did some rituals. I will describe what happened and adjust with my therapist."

Avoid:

"I ruined the exposure."

There is no benefit in converting treatment into all-or-nothing scoring.

When a New Theme Appears

"New content, possible old mechanism. I will tell my clinician if the change matters, and I will not conduct a private trial."

If there are new red flags, treat them as new clinical information.

If only the subject changed, the familiar response may still fit.

When You Are Tempted to Stop Medication Because of a Scary Story

"I am worried about what I read. I will contact my prescriber before changing the medication."

Then stop searching for a private verdict.

A medication question belongs with the clinician who can review the specific medicine and your circumstances.

When You Are Afraid to Start Medication

"I want to understand the benefits, risks, alternatives, uncertainty, and the risks of untreated symptoms. I am not asking for a zero-risk promise."

That is an informed-consent question.

When You Think You Should Be Better by Now

"What behavior is freer than it was a month ago?"

Maybe thoughts still occur.

If you are avoiding less, ritualizing less, disclosing more accurately, or using care more normally, those changes matter.

If behavior is worsening, contact treatment.

Do not use an arbitrary recovery deadline as a verdict.

When Someone Says, "Every Mother Has Weird Thoughts"

You can answer:

"Some intrusive thoughts are common. Mine are causing repeated compulsions and interfering with care, so I am getting assessed."

This avoids two extremes.

You do not have to accept dismissal.

You also do not have to prove that your thought is uniquely terrible.

When Someone Says, "How Could You Think That?"

"That is why I am getting professional help. The thought is unwanted, and I need you not to judge the content before you understand the clinical pattern."

If the person is not part of your care, you can end the conversation.

Privacy is allowed.

When You Need a Second Opinion

"I understand your current assessment. Because OCD is a concern and the harm content is difficult to distinguish, I would like to know whether a perinatal mental health or OCD specialist can review the case."

A second opinion is not guaranteed in every system.

Ask what route exists.

When You Need More Intensive Care

"I am not managing basic functioning with the current plan. What higher level of support is available?"

Be specific.

"I cannot complete infant care."

"I am not eating."

"I have not slept despite opportunity."

"I am having suicidal thoughts."

"I cannot control the rituals."

Severity is not a personal failure.

It changes what care may be appropriate.

When the Emergency Threshold Is Met

Use direct language.

"I have an intention to harm myself or the baby."

"I have a plan."

"I am hearing a voice telling me to act."

"I am severely confused."

"I have not slept and I feel unusually energized and unlike myself."

"I cannot keep us safe."

Then seek urgent professional assessment.

Do not soften the sentence because you are afraid of the consequence.

At that moment, getting the correct level of care is the priority.

When the Hard Hour Ends

Do not conduct a postmortem.

You do not need to decide whether you responded perfectly.

Ask one question:

"What is the next real task?"

Drink water.

Rest.

Feed the baby.

Take medication as prescribed.

Text the therapist about a scheduled matter.

Let your partner take over a shift.

Return to the day.

Language is useful when it moves you toward care and away from ritual.

Once it has done that job, you can stop talking about the thought.

References

American College of Obstetricians and Gynecologists. (2023). *Treatment and management of mental health conditions during pregnancy and postpartum: ACOG Clinical Practice Guideline No. 5. Obstetrics & Gynecology, 141*, 1262-1288. https://doi.org/10.1097/AOG.0000000000005202

American Psychiatric Association. (2022). *Diagnostic and statistical manual of mental disorders* (5th ed., text rev.). American Psychiatric Association Publishing.

Fairbrother, N., Collardeau, F., Albert, A. Y. K., Challacombe, F. L., Thordarson, D. S., Woody, S. R., & Janssen, P. A. (2021). High prevalence and incidence of obsessive-compulsive disorder among women across pregnancy and the postpartum. *The Journal of Clinical Psychiatry, 82*(2), 20m13398. https://doi.org/10.4088/JCP.20m13398

Hudak, R., & Wisner, K. L. (2012). Diagnosis and treatment of postpartum obsessions and compulsions that involve infant harm. *The American Journal of Psychiatry, 169*(4), 360-363. https://doi.org/10.1176/appi.ajp.2011.11050667

Hudepohl, N., MacLean, J. V., & Osborne, L. M. (2022). Perinatal obsessive-compulsive disorder: Epidemiology, phenomenology, etiology, and treatment. *Current Psychiatry Reports, 24*(4), 229-237. https://doi.org/10.1007/s11920-022-01333-4

International OCD Foundation. (n.d.). *Exposure and response prevention (ERP).* https://iocdf.org/about-ocd/ocd-treatment-guide/erp/

International OCD Foundation. (n.d.). *How is perinatal OCD treated?* https://iocdf.org/perinatal-ocd/how-is-perinatal-ocd-treated/

International OCD Foundation. (n.d.). *Medication.* https://iocdf.org/about-ocd/ocd-treatment-guide/understanding-medication/

International OCD Foundation. (n.d.). *Perinatal OCD treatment.* https://iocdf.org/perinatal-ocd/for-clinical-providers/perinatal-ocd-treatment/

Mulcahy, M., Long, C., Morrow, T., Galbally, M., Rees, C., & Anderson, R. (2023). Consensus recommendations for the assessment and treatment of perinatal obsessive-compulsive disorder (OCD): A Delphi study. *Archives of Women's Mental Health, 26*(3), 389-399. https://doi.org/10.1007/s00737-023-01315-2

National Institute for Health and Care Excellence. (2014, updated). *Antenatal and postnatal mental health: Clinical management and service guidance (CG192).* https://www.nice.org.uk/guidance/cg192

Royal College of Psychiatrists. (2026). *Standards for community perinatal mental health services* (7th ed., 2026-2028). https://www.rcpsych.ac.uk/docs/default-source/improving-care/ccqi/quality-networks/perinatal/pqn-community-standards-7th-edition-2026-2028.pdf

Royal College of Psychiatrists. (n.d.). *Perinatal OCD.* https://www.rcpsych.ac.uk/mental-health/mental-illnesses-and-mental-health-problems/perinatal-ocd

Shafran, R., Thordarson, D. S., & Rachman, S. (1996). Thought-action fusion in obsessive compulsive disorder. *Journal of Anxiety Disorders, 10*(5), 379-391. https://doi.org/10.1016/0887-6185(96)00018-7

Toor, R., Wiese, M., Croicu, C., & Bhat, A. (2024). Postpartum psychosis: A preventable psychiatric emergency. *Focus, 22*(1), 44-52. https://doi.org/10.1176/appi.focus.20230025

Wegner, D. M. (1994). Ironic processes of mental control. *Psychological Review, 101*(1), 34-52. https://doi.org/10.1037/0033-295X.101.1.34

About the Author

Maribel Quinn Dawson is a nonfiction writer focused on turning difficult, easily misunderstood mental health topics into plain, usable language. Her work draws on current clinical research and professional guidance while keeping diagnosis, risk assessment, and individual treatment decisions with qualified clinicians. She writes for readers who need precision without euphemism and practical steps without false guarantees.

www.ingramcontent.com/pod-product-compliance
Lightning Source LLC
LaVergne TN
LVHW010714061126
851857LV00014B/1180
* 9 7 8 1 9 1 1 8 3 8 7 3 9 *